M·A·I·N·E
F·A·R·M
A YEAR OF COUNTRY LIFE

M·A·I·N·E
F·A·R·M

A YEAR OF COUNTRY LIFE

Stanley Joseph and Lynn Karlin

Random House

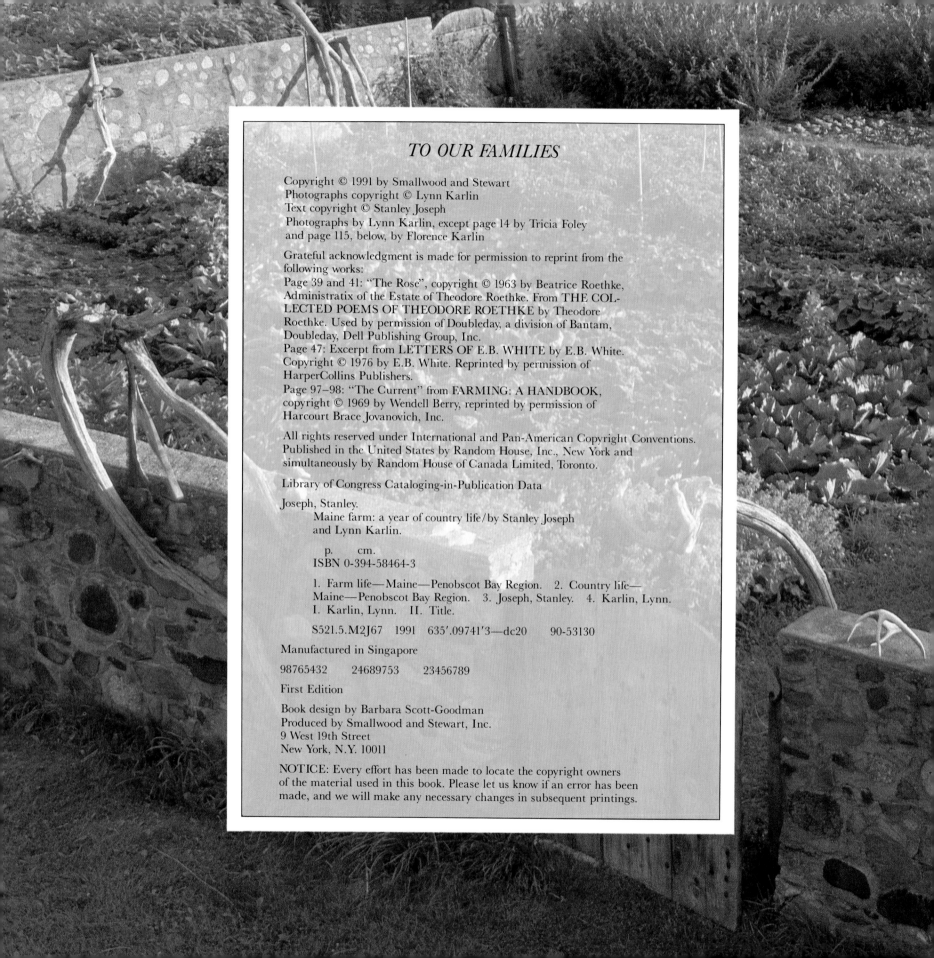

TO OUR FAMILIES

Grateful acknowledgment is made for permission to reprint from the
following works:
Page 39 and 41: "The Rose", copyright © 1963 by Beatrice Roethke,
Administratix of the Estate of Theodore Roethke. From THE COL-
LECTED POEMS OF THEODORE ROETHKE by Theodore
Roethke. Used by permission of Doubleday, a division of Bantam,
Doubleday, Dell Publishing Group, Inc.
Page 47: Excerpt from LETTERS OF E.B. WHITE by E.B. White.
Copyright © 1976 by E.B. White. Reprinted by permission of
HarperCollins Publishers.
Page 97–98: "The Current" from FARMING: A HANDBOOK,
copyright © 1969 by Wendell Berry, reprinted by permission of
Harcourt Brace Jovanovich, Inc.

Library of Congress Cataloging-in-Publication Data

Joseph, Stanley.
    Maine farm: a year of country life/by Stanley Joseph
and Lynn Karlin.

    p.   cm.
    ISBN 0-394-58464-3

    1. Farm life—Maine—Penobscot Bay Region. 2. Country life—
Maine—Penobscot Bay Region. 3. Joseph, Stanley. 4. Karlin, Lynn.
I. Karlin, Lynn. II. Title.

    S521.5.M2J67 1991 635'.09741'3—dc20   90-53130

Manufactured in Singapore

98765432   24689753   23456789

First Edition

Book design by Barbara Scott-Goodman
Produced by Smallwood and Stewart, Inc.
9 West 19th Street
New York, N.Y. 10011

"I have an indestructible conviction that houses become in time stamped with the character of their owners. There is a kind of aura about every house I have ever lived in—so strong that I believe I could tell you a great deal about the owners after ten minutes spent within the walls—whether the wife was dominant, whether the family was happy or unhappy, and almost exactly the degree of education and culture and knowledge of the person who built and furnished and lived in it. In short, for me there are few things in life more interesting and revealing than the houses in which people live."

Louis Bromfield,
Pleasant Valley

FOREWORD

Stanley Joseph and Lynn Karlin have put their mark on the house in which Scott and I lived for twenty-five years, as did we in our time. Scott and I were square, simple-living, subsistence farmers on the land which they now own and occupy. They have a flair for the fantastic and the photographic. They heartily enjoy life together on the farm and keep it flourishing in food and flower products.

Not that Scott and I didn't have a wonderful time building and working at it together. We did, but there was little frolicking in our lives. We were staid, systematic, and scheduled in comparison with Lynn and Stan. It was an old, decrepit place when we took it over in 1951. We tinkered a bit with it, adding a fireplace, a balcony, and a woodshed, but never attempting very much in the way of renovation. Scott dug, by hand, and carted away, by wheelbarrow, thousands of loads of swamp muck to create the pond back of the house and to build up the garden site. We enclosed the quarter-acre garden he created with a 5-foot-high stone wall, which took us fourteen years to build. We never intended the old house for our permanent home. We itched to build again in stone as we had in Vermont. Finally, in our 70s and 90s, on an adjacent plot of ground directly overlooking Penobscot Bay, we put up our final stone house.

Lynn and Stan garden and work on their place continually, adding to its appearance and utility. They have built up a business of making dried-flower wreaths, and they sell organic vegetables to nearby inns and restaurants. Stan works at basketry and has made an ingenious willow coracle to sail. The garden blooms not only with the greenery but with the scarecrows made from beach driftwood. Their six cats promenade on the garden walls. Their sauna is a meeting place for neighbors. Their stamp is on the place. I'm glad to see it blossom. May it continue to give them joy, and joy to future dwellers.

Helen Nearing

CAPE ROSIER

"It is the story of all life that is holy and it is good to tell, and of us two-leggeds sharing in it with the four-leggeds and the wings of the air and all green things; for these are children of one mother and their father is one Spirit."

—Black Elk

We live along the coast of Maine, on a 22-acre farm on Penobscot Bay within sight, sound, and smell of the sea, halfway up the 3,000-mile coastline between Kittery and Eastport, on the rocky shores of a small peninsula, Cape Rosier, an hour's drive from the nearest traffic light or shopping mall. Here we are regulated by the weather, the tides, the planting, nurturing, and harvesting of crops, and the dramatically different four seasons.

Returning from faraway travels, it is always comforting to cross the bridge connecting New Hampshire to Maine. There suddenly seem to be more trees and fewer cars, more space. Time seems to slow down as we leave Interstate 95 at Augusta and follow the meandering roads around dark, wooded lakeshores, past old Summer camps, weathered shingle cottages, down to the quaint villages with their white New England churches and the smell of the sea. The Cape Rosier turnoff is a scarcely traveled road that passes farms, blueberry barrens, old wooden houses with long white porches, dooryards piled high with lobster traps, before dwindling down to the dirt track that leads to our farm, down to the last six miles of winding roads and spruce- and fir-covered hills that have become so familiar to us, down to the tidal cove with the sea gulls and eider ducks, and at long last up the driveway to our farm and the quiet that goes with this place.

What led me to Cape Rosier and the Nearings' farm in 1975 was their book *Living the Good Life*, which had first appeared in 1954. I had read their account of homesteading on a Vermont farm while I was living in Europe, where I had my first experience with farm life on the Greek island of Skiathos. There I met Yannis Kandarakis, who farmed on the wild north side of the island with his four sons. To this day, their farm is the most beautiful I have ever seen. It begins in a steep valley lined with olive and orange groves and falls to the sea and a long sandy beach that looks toward Mt. Pelion and the Volos peninsula. In between

Still going strong at ninety-seven, Scott Nearing (top) used his favorite tool, the wheeled cultivator, to prepare the soil for Spring planting.

Raking hay, Helen Nearing (above) is healthy and vigorous in her eighties.

An aerial view of Orr Cove on Cape Rosier shows our farm (previous page).

are fields of tomatoes, eggplants, peppers, zucchini, melons sweeter than any I ever tasted, figs falling off the trees, and grapes. Yannis kept horses, sheep, and pigs and had the finest water on the island, water which gurgled out of a pipe near his house day and night. He fed himself and his family with the best of foods; he made his own cheese and wine, cured his own olives, dried figs, and caught octopus and squid by torchlight.

He said that, in exchange for several hours' work each morning, I could live on his land. Living on the farm gave me a chance to see firsthand the rhythms of farm life. It was a startling encounter with the simple and timeless values of self-sufficiency. I'd be up at 6 A.M. and have breakfast of yogurt and honey and a cup of strong coffee. I'd work from 8 to 11 and enjoy a huge lunch with the family; spend afternoons swimming, snorkeling, and fishing; and make a dinner of fresh vegetables, feta cheese, olives, and tomato salad, washed down with retsina.

That's about the time I read *Living the Good Life* by Helen and Scott Nearing. Their book, more than any other, changed my life. Scott, who had been a professor of economics at the Wharton School of Finance, had lost his job because of his radical politics and was blacklisted by other universities. In search of a simpler, more rewarding alternative to a system they perceived as founded on materialism and exploitation, the Nearings had taken over a run-down farm in a remote area of Vermont. The year was 1932, when Scott was forty-seven and Helen twenty years younger.

Living the Good Life described the more fundamental, balanced life of self-sufficiency and good health they achieved in the years that followed. The Nearings were practical people as well as philosophers, and in their book they explained how to garden organically, what could be done with all the food one grew, and how to live more in harmony with nature and with the community. They didn't make it sound easy, but they did show how to take more responsibility for what one did every day.

I returned to the United States in Spring 1975, determined to put into practice some of the ideas I had acquired in Europe. It was a struggle to readapt to the modern world. I could not shop in supermarkets for long because they seemed too big, impersonal, and filled with row upon endless row of junk food. So with Scott Nearing's phrase "how to live simply in a troubled world" still in my mind, I decided to search for the farm they had described in *Living the Good*

This is the house as it appeared when I bought it in 1980.

Life. When I found the Nearings' stone house in Vermont, a neighbor told me I was 300 miles off and 25 years late. Vermont, with its skiing industry, was getting too commercial, and the Nearings had moved to Harborside, Maine, in 1950.

In mid-August, I drove north and east through Vermont and New Hampshire into Maine. No one I met along the coast had ever heard of Harborside, but I found it on a map. Near Castine, it was about halfway up the coast on Cape Rosier, a tiny peninsula all but hidden away from busy Route 1. I remember being struck that first day by the purity of Cape Rosier and the farm, particularly of the light, which reminded me of Greece. It was the first spot since my stay on Yannis's farm where I felt I could live.

That day, Helen Nearing greeted me at their back door. She was seventy-two then, but her movements were those of a teenager. Ninety-two-year-old Scott came in from the garden soon after. Deeply wrinkled and tanned, he was strong and healthy and spoke with great clarity. He seemed to chuckle a lot. Their farm consisted of about twenty acres, with eight in fields, and an old Cape-style house overlooking the bay. Just to the west of the house was a small barn and Scott's

I harvest tomatoes from the walled garden in Summer.

workshop. Out back was a large, shallow pond with a small island in the middle. Scott's view of the pond was typical of an economist's. In his deep orator's voice, he told me about the 16,000-wheelbarrow loads of muck he took away to build it.

For weeks, I camped half a mile down the road with Eliot and Sue Coleman, early leaders of the organic farming movement. Every morning I joined fifteen or so other people in their twenties and thirties working in the Colemans' lush and exciting vegetable gardens. We all ate lunch together, a ragged band of aspiring back-to-the-landers, taking turns preparing hearty meals of buckwheat, peanut butter, and fresh vegetables and joining in lively discussions about everything from horses to rotary tillers to politics to seaweed. There seemed to be a good feeling of community in this little group, and it was very reluctantly that I left, continuing up the coast in search of a farm of my own.

Three years later, I returned to Harborside and learned that Helen and Scott were selling their old place. I went to visit them, and Helen told me, when I asked about the farm, "Oh, you're number 42." But two years later, my offer was accepted, and in June 1980, I moved in. In what would be their last project

together, Scott and Helen had built a new stone house next door, and we agreed to share their old garden for that first Summer while they built up the soil and finished the stone walls of their new garden.

The Nearings had been a major influence behind my decision to live in the country, but now I was actually taking on the 100-year-old farmhouse and the gardens where they had spent their last thirty years. I had ambition, but not a vast amount of experience, and I wasn't at all sure if I could earn enough to keep the place going. I hoped to earn my living growing and selling vegetables—I could expand the gardens and sell the produce—and the highbush blueberries could bring in some money as a cash crop. I had a neighbor, Wendell Davis, rotary-till a patch of new ground on which I hoped to grow strawberries, another cash crop. Not sure if the yield would be sufficient, I asked him if the area was large enough. "Never plant more than the wife can pick" was his advice. I didn't tell him I didn't have a wife.

In the first years, I came close to failing. There was far too much work for a single person, or maybe even two people, to do, and the house, barn, shed, and

I make willow baskets with Lynn in the yard in front of the house in Spring.

greenhouse all needed repairs. The Summer of 1981, I used to drive around Cape Rosier each Saturday morning, selling a lettuce here, a few quarts of blueberries there. In July 1982 I met Lynn Karlin, my future wife. She had set out with a friend from Holland to meet the Nearings. Arriving at Helen's place too early for visiting hours, Lynn drove farther up the road, encountered my vegetable sign, and came up the driveway. From the start the chemistry was right, and we did have a lot in common. Lynn had worked in New York City as a freelance photographer for thirteen years and cherished hopes of being able to move to the country. She had worked on a kibbutz in Israel after college and felt that she wanted to live on a farm one day, and in June 1983 she moved in. Though we had limited experience, we made up for it with energy and determination. That first Summer together, we expanded the vegetable business and started selling wreaths of dried flowers, which continues, along with Lynn's photography, to be our main source of income today.

Adjusting to the country was not difficult for Lynn. She liked the feeling of security and inner peace that living in a small town offers, plus the expansive feeling of being able to try new things that she wouldn't have had time or energy for in the big city, such as flying. In fact, in 1988, Lynn got her pilot's license. She likes the small, uncontrolled gravel-strip airport, the camaraderie among the pilots, and flying along such a spectacular coastline with its hundreds of islands. She's even taken up delivering fresh vegetables by plane to an inn on a nearby island. She enjoys feeling the soil under her bare feet and getting up in the morning and jumping in the pond in the Summer. Like me, she enjoys continuing many of the timeless rituals that are part of living on the land. Here we can appreciate the cycles of the seasons—eagerly anticipating the first asparagus and rhubarb or early Spring flowers, enjoying an outing in the kayak on a Summer evening or eating a fresh-picked Summer salad, watching the Fall leaves turn colors before our eyes, and walking out after the first snowstorm, going cross-country skiing, or ice-skating under the glow of the full moon in the brisk Winter air.

Over the years, with the help of our neighbors and friends, we have made major repairs to the old house and barn, torn down the rotted half of the greenhouse, expanded the pond, and built a sauna. We have only just completed our final repairs, but there are still plenty more projects we'd like to do: moving the woodshed around to the north side of the house and replacing it with a greenhouse on the south side, building a screened porch on the house, and converting an old shed to a darkroom. We have lots of plans, but everything always seems to take much longer than we anticipate. Work on our farm takes up most of our time from March, when we start the plants, until late November, when we stop making wreaths and work on next year's firewood, cleaning up fallen trees in the woods, and gather in the seaweed left on the beach after big storms. Every Winter we like to travel, and we escape the cold of Harborside for a couple of months. Half the time we spend in New York City and the other half in a warm place such as Bali or Mexico. We feel very fortunate to have found a home in this community and to have constructed a life in which we have the freedom to carry on our work in a creative way.

M aine Spring is a long, slow, tantalizing unfolding. People who live closer to the sun cannot imagine how those of us in Maine look forward to uncovering the first shoots of life under a heavy mulch of hay or how we appreciate each small increment in our measure of light. At either end of the Spring season, we experience sensory extremes. Spring begins in lonely silence broken only by the sounds of the sea and culminates in a burst of bird song amidst luxuriant growth. Leaving Winter, we begin and end our days shivering in the icy dark, but by the time of the Summer solstice the northern light is warming both ends of the day and the short Summer nights make up for the tardiness of Spring.

Goog Bakemen, a storekeeper in West Brooksville, warned me several years ago about the last days of the long Maine Winter. In a deep, raspy voice, he told me, "If the old folks here can make it up 'March Hill,' they'll make it through another year." Even in late March, Winter does not give up its grip on the Maine coast easily, and the struggle seems to intensify as underground the process of renewal begins almost unseen.

The ice won't be off the pond until mid-April, but already the deftly camouflaged peepers, *Hyla crucifer*, have begun their primeval chorus. Generally, we're due for at least one more snowstorm and many more cold and windy days before the month is over. By the beginning of May, the hillsides are lightly carpeted with a fresh growth of grass and dotted here and there with the golden heads of the season's first dandelions. Then out come the lawn mowers, the leaves on the trees—and the blackflies. But these little dark scourges of the crisp northern air cannot deter us from the timeless good feeling that comes with breaking out an old oiled mitt and playing softball again, going barefoot in the garden, or dashing naked into the pond.

May is a vibrant time of year on the coast of Maine. Suddenly the ferns unfurl, the skunk cabbage is a foot high, and there is enough rhubarb ripened for a first pie. We can see and hear the changes of Spring almost daily. Yet the temperature is still only a chilly 42 degrees Fahrenheit. In some years, because of cold winds and rains, we don't see daffodils or transplant our tomato seedlings or celebrate May Day until the end of the month.

In late March, we remove the two feet of Winter mulch from the walled vegetable garden. Here, Lynn is taking a wheelbarrow loaded with Jerusalem artichoke stalks and mulch hay to the compost pile (above).

The Maine coast can be inundated with a heavy snowstorm as late as April (opposite). Though Winter's snow tends to linger, the underground process of renewal begins unseen.

March 21

Although Spring officially begins today, this year the ground is still frozen. The normal temperature for this time of year is about 37 degrees, but nighttime readings routinely fall into the 20s, with cold arctic winds blowing in from Canada to the northwest.

Nevertheless, there is already work to be done in the gardens. Just to the west of the barn is the 100-square-foot garden where the Nearings grew most of their produce, enclosed by a 5-foot-high stone wall that Helen and Scott built. We, too, grow many of our vegetables in this garden, and it is here that we begin removing the thick layer of mulch with which we covered the carrots last November. Two feet of hay has protected them sufficiently from freezing and thawing repeatedly during Winter so that they are in good shape. We have found that leaving the carrots in the colder temperatures of the ground instead of bringing them into the root cellar protects them from carrot-root maggots and results in less damage to the crop, and now we are able to gather enough carrots to last us until early Summer.

Today we also removed the fir branches that have protected the perennial flowers from the severe temperature fluctuations of Winter. But this year, because of the lack of additional insulating snow cover, the frost went especially deep, and we found that we have lost many of our plantings of sage and baby's breath, and even the new growth of some of the artemisias. We burned the fir branches we gathered up before the frost went out of the ground—this is the safest time to burn brush. This Spring burning seems an ancient rite: to be done with the old and welcome in the new; to banish evil spirits and rekindle the earth's reproductive cycle. Too often we let such traditions die out. The essayist E. B. White, who lived not far from here, wrote about the decline of such rituals, "The first day of Spring was once a time for taking young virgins into the fields, there in dalliance to set an example for nature to follow. Now we just set the clocks ahead an hour and change the oil in the crankcase." Modern practicality notwithstanding, in no other season is our sense of ancient ritual so deep.

March 29

Yesterday, while I was in the barn starting seeds, I heard a distant but unmistakable honking sound and I yelled to Lynn. She came running and we were able to witness the timeless, wondrous sight of Canada geese in a huge formation heading northeast—there must have been over sixty of them in a loose V. Migratory birds follow the Maine coast and begin arriving in our area in mid-March, with many of them continuing on to Newfoundland, Labrador, and Greenland. In Spring, Penobscot Bay is a bird-watcher's paradise. A few days earlier we had seen the first robins of the year and a male purple finch with raspberry-colored plumage at the bird feeder by the kitchen window. Three hundred species of birds visit Maine every year, though just sixty are year-round residents. In part, it must be the abundant insect life and the relatively moderate temperatures typical of New England in Spring and Summer that cause so many species to make such a long flight. The border of the Atlantic Ocean constitutes the main thoroughfare for the migration of most eastern land species and is almost the only route for aquatic birds. Along this route, unusual landmarks, particularly prominent elevations, serve as guides and rallying points. The granite-peaked Mount Desert Island, about forty miles to the east, is a most important landmark for birds migrating along the eastern seaboard.

Scientists now know that bird migration paths do not depend on any single cue, relying instead on a variety of information sources. Visual cues, the most obvious of which are topographical landmarks such as mountains or bays, serve as navigational guides, but apparently even individual trees serve as guideposts. Equally fascinating is the bird's ability to orient itself according to the position of the sun, which is especially important for long-distance migrations. Recent studies with homing pigeons suggest that the earth's magnetic field also provides an important reference for orientation. It is a mystery and a miracle to me that I can walk out in the woods and be lost in fifteen minutes, whereas the arctic tern can fly 20,000 miles between the arctic and the antarctic and not get lost.

Canada geese follow the Maine coast as they make their annual migration north. Seeing their V-shaped formation, which can be as early as mid-March, is a sure sign for us that Spring is coming.

A great stillness envelops the pond and our sauna as coastal fog keeps us locked in during the long gray days of early Spring.

STARTING SEEDLINGS

*E*very year beginning in late March, we start thousands of vegetable and flower seedlings, which we then transplant outdoors in our gardens. When growing several thousand plants each year, we have found that it is far more economical to grow from seed. But almost as importantly, we are able to grow a far wider range of plants than we could if we relied on commercially raised seedlings. Gardening is so much a process of trial and error; we enjoy the chance to experiment with new varieties from the many seed catalogs.

Nearly all the seedlings have their beginnings in the kitchen on a table near the wood stove where we can maintain the constant warm temperature necessary for their germination. This year we started four varieties of tomatoes, early, late, cherry, and plum; several types of peppers, from green to yellow to red and sweet and semi-hot; eggplant, celery, and parsley; dozens of flowers for drying, the most important of which is statice, which we grow in five different colors; and also *Celosia, Helichrysum* or straw flowers, *Helipterum, Xeranthemum, Salvia hormonium, Salvia victoria*, globe amaranth, *Ammobium*, two varieties of *Nigella*, and *Scabiosa stellata*, grown for its domelike seed pods.

For our cut flowers, we usually start three different varieties of asters; snapdragons; several varieties of zinnias; rudbeckia; cosmos; calendula; three varieties of dahlias from dwarf to giant 5-foot-high varieties; blue lace flower or *Trachymene caerulea*, which is a wonderfully subtle flower; cleome in pink and white; and *Centaurea cyanus* or bachelor buttons. As these seeds sprout and are removed from the sprouting table, we make room for other flowers such as petunias, lobelia, and allysum, and herbs—basil, thyme, coriander, oregano, sage, hyssop, and dill.

We start seedlings in peat containers (5 inches by 7 inches) filled with a moistened soilless potting mixture (developed at Cornell University) that contains horticultural sphagnum moss, horticultural vermiculite, and perlite. Mineral aggregates such as vermiculite and perlite make the soil more porous so water soaks rapidly into and through the mix and keeps the roots well aerated. Soilless potting mixtures also have the advantage of being sterile, which reduces the incidence of soilborne diseases such as damping off, a fungus that attacks seedlings. These mixtures hold about 8 times their weight in water.

I spread several seeds thinly over the top of each container and cover them with a very thin layer of the potting mix, tamping it down so that the seeds make good contact with the mixture. One of the most common mistakes is sowing too deeply. A seed has only enough food within itself for a limited period of growth, and a tiny seed sown too deeply soon expends that energy and dies before it can reach the surface. In each container, I also include a label noting what I've planted and the date of planting.

In order to retain moisture, we cover each container with a piece of glass or plastic wrap. We've found that most seeds sprout best at temperatures between 68 and 72 degrees Fahrenheit. If the temperature is too low, the seed takes up water but cannot germinate and therefore rots; if it is too high, the seed's growth is also prevented. Lynn and I check the pots daily, and as soon as the seeds break the surface, we remove the covering and relocate them under fluorescent lights. "Grow lights" are not necessary; instead we

use ordinary 4-foot-long "shop lights" hung 4 to 6 inches above the seedlings. To encourage better and slower growth at this stage and to keep the plants from getting spindly or leggy, it is best to keep them at temperatures in the low 60s.

Because we grow so many plants, not all of them can be started simultaneously, so the process of sowing, sprouting, and transferring the pots under lights extends over several weeks during the Spring. As the first containers are removed to grow under lights, new seedlings are begun.

About ten days after the first seeds sprout, they begin to develop their first true leaves, signaling the time to prick them out of their pots and transplant them into flats. Each flat usually contains 50 individual units, which I fill with premoistened soilless potting medium. Grouping the plants together in these flats simplifies watering and fertilizing and gives us the best control over their growth. In addition, since a 10-inch-by-20-inch flat contains 50 units, it conserves valuable space in growing areas. Using an ordinary kitchen fork, I loosen the seedlings, taking care not to damage the tender stems and roots; in fact, it's best to handle the seedlings by their leaves. With a pencil, I poke a hole in each unit of the flat and gently drop the seedling into its new home, taking care to firm it in.

The seedlings continue to grow under lights on a home-built three-tiered structure we refer to as "the hotel." The hotel is built of 2-inch-by-2-inch uprights, with sides 1 inch by 3 inches. Overall, it is 50 inches high and 60 inches long. The distance between each tier is 14 inches. Two 4-foot-long shop lights are hung side by side on chains on each level. By holding four trays on each level, the hotel saves us a great deal of space—at least 600 plants can be raised in that fairly small area. All the lights are controlled by one timer which goes on at 6 A.M. and shuts off at 8 P.M. This year we added a temporary greenhouse to the south side of the living room to take advantage of the warmth from

the wood-heated room and the sun, and this structure held another 12 flats.

By the end of March, our permanent greenhouse, which is located at the sheltered southwest-facing corner of the walled garden, will be getting warm—in the 60s to 70s on sunny days and above freezing at night, and we can safely sprout the hardier crops such

as lettuce, radicchio, mustard, bok choy, onions, leeks, bunching onions, and arugula there.

By late April, the seedlings are well established in the house—about two to three inches high. To accommodate the increasing number of sprouted seedlings, we start to relocate them to the unheated greenhouse to begin the long hardening-off process. These

seedlings require constant monitoring to make sure that they are watered and fertilized properly and that there are no problems with aphids, slugs, or damping off. We've found it best to water them as infrequently as possible—about every fourth day. Every other fourth day, or every eighth day, we add a water-soluble fertilizer. In late April, the red and

green lettuce—a loose-leaf variety—and other hardy crops are moved from the greenhouse to be protected under plastic tunnels, which are left open in the daytime and closed at night to protect the plants from frosts.

By early May, we can transplant the arugula, lettuce, and collard greens into the walled garden. Each of the 50 plants contained in a flat is popped out and dipped in a diluted mixture of seaweed and sea fish emulsion with a good blend of trace minerals and a ratio of 5:2:2 parts per 100 of nitrogen, phosphorous, and potash to give them a good start.

Nearly all our seedlings are transplanted to the gardens in mid- to late May, when the soil has warmed up and the danger of frost has passed. We prepare the soil in advance of transplanting. It takes two to three weeks for the turned-in winter rye to break down enough for new planting to begin; prior to tilling, we are constantly monitoring the soil. Our test is simple: We take a handful of dirt, squeeze it into a ball, and drop it from waist level. If it breaks apart on impact, it's dry enough to till.

During the growing season we use every single space in our garden intensively. By staggering our planting, we not only make optimum use of the garden, but also have crops continuously for the longest possible time. As soon as one plant is picked, another takes its place. So beginning in late March, we start 150 new lettuce plants in flats each week, and as of June 1, we increase that number to 250 and continue at this rate until mid-August. The plants spend about a month in the flats and another month in the garden.

Relying on previous years' maps of the gardens, we are careful to rotate crops. Different botanical families take different nutrients out of the soil and attract different insects and soil-born diseases. Some, like legumes, add nitrogen to the soil. Where last year's peas and beans grew, this year will go the lettuce and other leafy salad crops.

In the first years on the farm, I used a hand-pushed cultivator to break up the earth for planting (top). Today, with a much larger area under cultivation, I use a rotary tiller (above) to prepare the soil for cover crops, and now I use the cultivator only for light work.

April 4

The warming days have resulted in the thawing and breaking up of the earth. We escaped a bad mud season because of the lack of snow, but the deep frost produced heaves in the roads and it took a strong stomach to drive the 20 miles to Blue Hill, the picturesque New England town where we get most of our supplies. The frost must work its way out of the ground before the earth can dry out and the bumps disappear.

We began the annual pruning of the highbush blueberries. These berries were planted by the Nearings in the 1960s on a gentle slope to the southeast of the house, covering about a quarter of an acre and fenced in by 8-foot-high chicken wire. The cats joined us as we worked, often climbing on our backs to provide a furry collar against the chill winds. They love to sniff out mouse holes and occasionally pounce on a fat field mouse or race up the cedar poles that the Nearings had put up to support the fishnets they used to protect the fruit from hungry birds. Helen says that the effort to put up those nets every year was among her worst moments on the farm. I can understand. In 1980 I managed to cover the berries with netting, but some birds got in anyway and gorged themselves before becoming frantic to get out. Thereafter, I dispensed with the netting and we now share our berries with the birds.

A blueberry bush produces fruit on wood from the previous season's growth. The largest fruit is borne on the most vigorous wood. Most varieties tend to overbear, and unless some of the buds are pruned off, the berries become relatively small, with too little strong new growth for the next season. Using pruning shears, we start by cutting away all dead growth and weak branches. The bushes are frequently attacked by witches' broom, a mass of branches— caused by a fungi or a virus—that entwine the plants. These branches must also be removed and then burned along with the prunings. Each Spring we think the old bushes are on their last legs, but then come August they give us anywhere from 500 to 600 quarts to sell and plenty for blueberry pie and ice cream.

April 22

We have been enjoying the nightly peeper concert since the beginning of April, when these tiny creatures resumed their noisy chorus around the pond. Any day now sounds like broken banjo strings will accompany the peeper chorus,

During the long Winter layoff, the garden tools are in their place (above), ready for Spring use.

Willows harvested for baskets (left) are best cut from late Fall until early Spring before the sap rises, to allow for faster drying of the material.

So much needs to be done in early Spring, despite the foggy damp and chill, even when the ground is still frozen. We prune some of the buds off the blueberry bushes (clockwise from upper left) to ensure large berries and abundant growth in the next season; we strip the apple trees of dead branches and suckers and then prune out branches in the centers to promote new, healthy growth; we remove the mulch that has protected our crop of winter carrots; and we burn the fir branches used as mulch to protect our perennials from severe Winter temperature fluctuations.

heralding the mating of the large green frog, *Rana clamitans*; and before long hundreds of thousands of tadpoles will emerge from their gelatinous egg masses.

Adult peepers are only about an inch in length. After transforming from a tadpole to a frog, a peeper takes three to four years to reach sufficient maturity to breed. The exuberant males call the females to come and mate. As the weather warms up, the peepers' call increases until sometimes we feel we're in the midst of a vast jungle. Henry Beston describes it in his book, *Northern Farm, A Chronicle of Maine*, "Heard nearby, the din . . . is nearly deafening. It is a Dionysian ecstasy of night and Spring, a shouting and a rejoicing out of puddles and streams, a festival of belief in sheer animal existence." Sometimes at night Lynn and I try to see how close we can get to the thousands of calling peepers, but they suddenly become aware of us and the entire pond becomes as still as a monastery.

It is time to prune the apple and pear trees. There is great satisfaction in clipping the soft shoots of new growth from the branches of an apple tree. Using a pruning saw and pruning shears, I remove all the dead branches and suckers, which shoot up along well-established branches, and prune out interlacing branches to open the center of the tree to light and air, a step that enhances the general health of the tree. An apple tree not pruned will develop too many branches and stunted fruit. Most of the older trees on our farm bear apples that are not much good for eating, but they do make a pungent and tasty cider.

As soon as the weather starts to get warm, we divide and replant many perennials. Here, Lynn is separating some yarrow plants.

April 25

There is a saying in Maine that "if you don't like the weather, wait five minutes." This better describes Spring in Maine than any other time of year. Yesterday was sunny and calm; the temperature reached as high as 60 degrees. It was the first day that the pond was free of the Winter ice it had worn since November. Now suddenly it was transformed into a pool of fresh water, soon to be teeming with peepers, tadpoles, green frogs, bullfrogs, water bugs, dragonflies, mosquitoes, and blackflies. The earth had dried out sufficiently for us to do our first rotary tilling on a patch of winter rye inside the walled garden. The rye was about six inches high, and it was good to feel the tines of the tiller sink into the earth and begin breaking up this verdant and densely planted cover crop.

Inspired by the warm temperatures, Lynn and I launched the wooden raft on our pond. We felt like a couple of Huck Finns poling the simple raft about the

Fiddlehead ferns (Matteuccia struthiopteris) *are a delight to watch in Spring as they grow taller and unfurl their feathery bodies. Growing in damp, shady places near brooks, edible ones should be picked before they reach five or six inches high. They are delicious steamed until they are bright green or can be pierced with a sharp knife. Their flavor is something like mild asparagus. Just squeeze on some lemon and top the fiddleheads with a pat of butter.*

water. Two of our six cats joined in the expedition, having also caught a bit of Spring fever. Late this afternoon we took all the cats on a walk down to Orr Cove, which faces northwest toward the Camden Hills in the distance. When the tide is out, the cove has a great expanse of beach, and relishing the salty air, the cats chased one another across the shore, among the crab claws, sand dollars, sea urchins, and whelk, clam, and mussel shells—a seafood lover's paradise.

About fifty yards out on the water, Lynn and I spied a pair of eider ducks. Soon a flock of young would be trailing behind them, and the parents would be keeping a wary eye out for their great enemy, the black-backed sea gull. The common eider (*Somateria mollisima*) is the largest duck in the Penobscot Bay area, and the male is easily recognizable by its black underpart and white back, breast, and head. The female is a mottled brown. Eider ducks are best known for their down, the very soft feathers the female plucks from her breast to line her nest. Nesting on the ground and often in colonies, the eider duck lays her eggs close to the shore. In Norway and Iceland, some eider colonies are fenced in, and the down is gathered from the nest a few days before hatching, without adverse effect on the species. The eider duck population in this country was once in serious decline, but since better methods for collecting down were introduced after the turn of the century, their numbers have increased spectacularly along the Maine coast; they are once again nesting in large numbers. Their diet consists mostly of mussels and other shellfish, which they swallow whole and crush with powerful stomach muscles. Some tough stomach, I'd say.

Lynn and I stayed on the beach to watch the sunset at 7:13, when the distant hills became almost black, the sky blazed red and orange and purple, and heavy clouds built in the west, hinting of the unsettled weather to come. Before heading back to the house, we were excited to hear that native cry of the north, the laughing of the loons. We could just make out a pair of them about one hundred yards out in the bay.

But today as I gazed out the window toward the water, the landscape looked like one of those old glass paperweights of a snowy farm scene turned upside down, with huge snowflakes scattered everywhere. Normally, we can easily make out a few houses on the shore of the island of Islesboro, which is only four miles away from us by water, but today it was entirely out of sight. The

JERUSALEM ARTICHOKE PICKLES

◆

Even before the frost goes out of the ground, we begin harvesting Jerusalem artichokes. We save some to plant in May for next Spring's crop.

Jerusalem artichokes are neither from Jerusalem nor artichokes. In fact, the tubers of this native American perennial sunflower, *Helianthus tuberosus*, were cultivated by the Penobscot Indians. Introduced to Europe by early explorers, the plant became more popular there than here. The name is thought to be a corruption of the Italian, *girasole articiocco*, meaning sunflowers.

Eaten raw, Jerusalem artichokes taste very much like water chestnuts. Baked, they are much sweeter than potatoes, reminding me more of a cross between a potato and a turnip. Our favorite way of eating them is raw in salads. The English are said to prefer them boiled in milk, providing an excellent accompaniment to roast beef. Although it is possible to harvest the artichokes in November and store them in sand, we prefer to leave them in the ground. This method produces sweeter tubers, since the frost gets into them, and provides us with fresh produce in the Spring when there is little else to harvest.

Jerusalem artichokes are very valuable to diabetics because they contain no starch and store sugar in the form of insulin and levulose. They are one of the few vegetables which supply pantothenic acid, as well as Vitamins A and C, plus calcium. Each Spring, we give away a good supply to encourage others to grow them, but always with the admonition to plant them in a separate patch because they are almost impossible to eradicate.

◆

2 cups cider vinegar

2 cups water

1/2 cup sugar

1/3 cup pickling salt

2 cloves garlic, coarsely chopped

1 1/2 to 1 3/4 pounds Jerusalem
    artichokes

◆

1. In a 2- or 3-quart nonreactive (nonaluminum) saucepan, stir together the vinegar, water, sugar, salt, and garlic. Bring to a boil.

2. Meanwhile, scrub the artichokes, but do not peel them. Slice them 1/4-inch thick and fill sterilized jars with the slices. (Use six 1/2-pint or three 1-pint jars.)

3. Pour the boiling pickling solution over the artichokes, being sure they are completely covered. A low-acid vegetable, it should be canned carefully according to manufacturer's directions. Seal and wait two weeks to open.

Yield: 3 pints

*B*ug season is at its worst during late Spring, when the ground is still damp and the air is getting warm. When planting lettuce, which we do continuously from late April to the end of August, a bug net is obligatory.

*T*he Holy Mackerels, our coed softball team, meets in Blue Hill and plays from mid-May into October. Here, Susan Hawkins takes a mighty swing (right).

temperature had dropped to 37 degrees, the wind was blowing a gale, and the scene was more like December than one month after the Spring equinox. In our garden all the tender shoots and buds that in the sunshine yesterday seemed full of promise are exposed to wintry blasts. April truly is the cruelest month.

May 10

We are at last getting some fine, warm days. The Holy Mackerels, a coed softball team that meets in Blue Hill and plays for the fun of it on Friday evenings, had its first outing. From the bench I could see that the left fielder was performing a modern dance called "swatting blackflies." This is just the beginning of the blackfly season, and already I can't wait for the last of them. Our pond temperature is up in the 50s now and on most days we dash into it for a quick, refreshing dip. There's nothing like it to ease the bug bites and rejuvenate the spirit. The white-throated sparrow calls out its sweet song from a clump of birch trees out back. Even more pleasing to us, tree swallows will dart and swoop about the pond, dining on blackflies. They say a swallow will eat its weight in bugs every day; I can't wait for them to start.

It is the female blackfly that after mating seeks nourishment—first nectar, then blood—for her eggs. She can fly ten miles or more, responding to large, high-contrast, brightly colored, or moving shapes. Once attracted, a combination of exhaled carbon dioxide and body heat stimulates her to land and bite. There are people who seldom get bitten, there are those who don't know they've been bitten until welts begin to form long after the fly has gone off to deposit her eggs, and there are those like me whose face, neck, and ears swell with "blackfly fever," especially early in the season. While gardening in blackfly season, especially on low-pressure, cloudy days, I wear my bug net, a mosquito-netted bonnet tied around the neck.

Rana clamitans, *the green frog (above), makes itself known with a low-pitched sound like a banjo string breaking.*

May 15

The golden yellow forsythia and daffodils have been out for a couple of weeks, and in a day or two the tulips will burst open. But it was a late Spring because of the great amount of rain—8 inches in the first two and a half weeks, which must be a record. In the five years that I have been keeping track of rainfall, rain in the entire month of May has ranged from a low of 2.5 inches in 1985 to a high of 4.7 inches in 1986.

The first dandelion flowers have bloomed in the back by the woodshed, and we have been picking young greens. The dandelion (*Taraxacum officinale*), also known in England as priest's crown or swine's snout, is considered by many lawn lovers to be a troublesome weed. Yet, it is welcomed by us. We boil the young leaves (old leaves are too bitter to be eaten) for about ten minutes, cool them in a colander, and add lemon juice, olive oil, and grated garlic for a delicious salad that I first tasted in Greece. The genus, *Taraxacum*, is derived from the Greek *taraxos* (disorder) and *akos* (pain); "official remedy" is a rough translation of the second Latin name, and the dandelion has, in fact, been widely used for its supposed health-giving properties. Together with spinach and chicory, for example, dandelion greens were found to make a fine Spring tonic for cleansing the intestines after a Winter diet heavy with potatoes. The root, which can often be a foot long and takes some serious digging, can also used as a coffee substitute. One year when I had foresworn caffeine I roasted the roots in the oven and then steeped them in water. I've since gone back to coffee.

Helen and Scott left behind some perennials in the walled garden—lovage, southern wood, delphinium, and comfrey—that have continued to thrive. Lovage (*Levisticum officinale*), an old English herb that is not so well known today, is one of the earliest plants to come up in Spring. We chop up the stalks for salads and use the leaves and stalks in our Spring soups; the taste is similar to but stronger than celery. Culpepper, the 17th-century English herbalist, tells us, "The distilled water is good for quinsey if the mouth and throat be gargled and washed therewith and the leaves bruised and fried with a little hog's lard and laid hot to any blotch or boil will quickly heal it."

The pond is warming up, and a hummingbird appeared, a harbinger of bustling activity. The days are longer; the sun rose around 4:45 and will set at 7:45 this evening. But this time of year there are a thousand things to do in these long daylight hours: the grass needs cutting, the gardens need rotary-tilling, perennials need weeding, field transplanting must be done now before the young plants become root bound, there's bread to bake, boats to paint.

The wild violets are out, and the *Houstonia* or tiny bluets and blue-eyed grasses, members of the Iris family, are flowering along the driveway. Just past the flagpole, where the hillside drops away to the bay, a clump of wild strawberries is in bloom. The rhubarb is growing rapidly, and soon we will be able to pull up the first fat reddish-green stalks. It was Scott Nearing who taught me that you don't cut rhubarb but rather, with two hands placed near the base of the stalk and a firm but gentle tugging action, dislocate it from its parent—a satisfying feeling when you get it right. Directly in front of the barn, the leaves on our twisted and gnarled old lilac tree, which the Nearings planted in the 1950s, are as big as mouse ears. *Wyman's Gardening Encyclopedia*, which many consider the bible of flowering plants, advises that perfect lilac blooms are normally expected only every other year, as often happens with woody plants.

May 28

We had almost ten inches of rain this month—a new record—forcing us to postpone our maypole dance several times. Finally, some strong sun dried out the fields, and we planned the dance for today. The celebration of May Day is supposed to have originated with the ancient Druids, who made immense fires on cairns in their worship of the god Bel. Other theories have it originating in

India, Egypt, and Rome, but in all cultures it represents a form of nature worship, welcoming Spring. The maypole was originally a mass of branches or a tree; we use a flagpole. On the appointed substitute day, Gail Disney, a rag-rug weaver, tied together long, colorful streamers which we attached high up on the pole. Gail instructed the women and children in the art of maypole dancing. The musicians warmed up and excitement built. Tom Hoey, Gail's husband, was our Lord of the Forest and Fecundity. Gail and I constructed his treelike costume by wiring together four willow hoops of widening diameter. The top ring rested on his head and the bottom fell near his knees. We wove freshly cut balsam fir branches through the hoops and attached two fierce-looking Balinese masks to the front and back at face level. To let us know that Spring was here and it was time to dance, to shake the spells, and to rise up like the sap in the trees, Tom rang a Swiss cowbell and growled fiercely. The dancers faced one another, the fiddle and whistle music began, and the women and children, skirts flowing in the breeze, danced around the pole, wrapping it in the colorful fabric. After-wards, out came the rhubarb wine and hard cider as the music and frolicking continued. As the sun set over Penobscot Bay, we gathered by the maypole and I read Theodore Roethke's poem "The Rose":

> There are those to whom place is unimportant,
> But this place, where sea and fresh water meet,
> Is important—
> Where the hawks sway out into the wind,
> Without a single wingbeat,
> And the eagles sail low over the fir trees,
> And the gulls cry against the crows
> In the curved harbors,
> And the tide rises up against the grass
> Nibbled by sheep and rabbits.
> . . . I sway outside myself
> Into the darkening currents,
> Into the small spillage of driftwood,
> The waters swirling past the tiny headlands.
> Was it here I wore a crown of birds for a moment

The maypole is wrapped (above) by the dancers with long, colorful cotton streamers.

*O*ur May Day celebration continues the ancient tradition of welcoming Spring with song and dance (opposite). Fiddlers play as dancers wrap the pole, and a mysterious spirit dressed in fir branches exhorts us to shake the Winter spells, to rise up like sap in the trees, and to dance. The ritual bread is baked in the outdoor, wood-fired, Quebec-style oven.

*B*y mid-May we can see the frothy white blossoms of the old apple trees over the garden wall (previous page).

While on a far point of rocks
The light heightened,
And below, in a mist out of nowhere,
The first rain gathered?
. . . And in this rose, this rose in the sea-wind,
Rooted in stone, keeping the whole of light,
Gathering to itself sound and silence—
Mine and the sea-wind's.

Accompanied by guitar and fiddle, we sang, our voices rising in the wind into a gentle howl, reminding us of ancient ways and lands of long ago. As the shadows lengthened, we headed to the island in the middle of the pond where our sauna stovepipe had been puffing out smoke for hours, preparing for our arrival. Slowly, we let the deep heat sink in, and we refreshed ourselves. Over and over, we plunged into the pond and returned to the sauna until we felt that lightness of being which comes with this bathing together, this deep cleansing shared among friends. Finally, we toasted the coming planting season—to fertility and healthy crops. And we turned to a delicious potluck supper of spinach and artichoke salad, potato-leek soup, great round loaves of sourdough rye bread, fresh herbed goat cheese, rhubarb pies, and cider and blueberry wine.

Myostis alpestris *(above) and pansy (below) are both early bloomers and add welcome color to the Spring garden.*

We fire up the sauna before our May dance so that we can relax in its welcoming heat after our festivities (opposite).

June 4

The dark green, shiny leaves of our early potatoes, Red Norlands, which we planted in early May, have broken the soil by a few inches, and it is time to put the winter or storage potatoes in. We have found that russets make the best baking potatoes, and we grow enough each year so that we can save a bushel for planting the following spring. With about fifty pounds of potatoes to a bushel, we can plant about three hundred row feet, which yields about five to seven bushels. Each year we rotate the potatoes around different gardens to try to prevent any soil-borne diseases from infecting the plants. But there's no fooling the flying Colorado potato beetle; every year we have serious problems with them.

Colorado potato beetles are among the most destructive and widespread garden pests in the United States. They feed on the foliage of tomatoes, potatoes, and eggplants, at times totally defoliating the plants. Some years we have lost

RHUBARB PIE

When rhubarb's bright red stalks emerge from the ground, we know that Spring is really here and that the days are warming up and getting longer. We pull up the rhubarb, throw the leaves in the compost, and make the first fresh pie of the year. I plan to use some of the rhubarb for wine, and Lynn cooks down a good amount to freeze.

We know Summer isn't far off when we eat our first fresh rhubarb pie (above).

In late May the fragrant blossoms of our blueberry bushes brighten our barn (opposite).

◆

4 cups young rhubarb, cut in half-inch pieces (1½ to 2 pounds)

1¼ cups sugar or 1 cup honey

⅓ cup crème de cassis (black-currant liqueur)

3 tablespoons quick-cooking tapioca

1 tablespoon grated lemon rind

Pastry for a double-crust 9-inch pie

◆

1. Preheat the oven to 450°F. In a large mixing bowl, thoroughly stir together the rhubarb, sugar, crème de cassis, tapioca, and lemon rind. Let the mixture stand 15 minutes.

2. Roll out half the pastry and ease it into a 9-inch pie pan. Spoon the rhubarb mixture into the shell. Cover the filling with the remaining pastry, either cut in lattice strips or as a solid top crust with several steam vents cut into it. Seal the top crust to the bottom and flute the edges.

3. Bake the pie 10 minutes, then lower the oven temperature to 350°F and bake an additional 40 minutes, until the filling is bubbly and the pastry is golden brown.

4. Cool the pie on a rack.

Yield: One 9-inch pie

Oriental poppies brighten the side of our house in late Spring (above and right).

Orange and yellow hawkweed and clover bloom in abundance in our lower field in early June (opposite).

On foggy days late in May, the intoxicating smell of lilacs pervades our yard (overleaf). Perfect lilac blooms are normally expected only every other year—as often happens with many woody plants.

half our crops to them. As they quickly develop immunity to many chemical pesticides, they are notoriously difficult to control. But because of a newly developed variety of *Bacillis thuringiensis*, or BT, we were looking forward to less of a problem with them. BT is an insect-infecting bacterium that has been used for years against such pests as cabbage loopers, tomato hornworms, mosquitoes, and corn earworms. Since its discovery in 1900, no insect targeted by any strain of the bacterium has ever built up any resistance to it. This new variety of botanical pesticide, "M-One," attacks the Colorado potato beetle and is harmless to humans, wildlife, and beneficial garden insects. Whenever possible, we use biological insecticides to control problem insects, and in most cases we have been able to. However, the tarnished plant bug, which attacks many of our flowers, has led us very reluctantly to use malathion on occasion. More recently, we have chosen to counter the damage caused by persistent pests by simply growing more flowers than we need. Usually, the bugs will attack weaker plants and leave more than enough strong, healthy flowers for us.

June 20

The rapid growth of Spring continues as we approach the Summer solstice, and harvesting has begun in earnest. It will be almost two months before we eat a tomato or an eggplant, but the zucchini plants, early potatoes, and peas are racing along and the delphiniums are only a couple weeks away from blooming. The chive flowers in the upper garden are in bloom—these are the first flowers we pick for our dried flower wreaths. We are also picking the first lettuce, spinach, bunching onions, rhubarb, and some columbine. As long as the days are, they aren't long enough to do what must be done. Around this time of year, I recall what E. B. White said about the commitment he made to his farm: "There is a strong likelihood that the country will be my undoing as I like it too well and take it too seriously. I have taken these 40 acres to be my bride, and of course that can be exhausting."

Exhausting, yes, but passion well-spent.

BUILDING THE SAUNA

I first became interested in saunas when I was in the army and was sent to East Berlin to photograph the May Day parade. I discovered a public sauna in West Berlin, an alluring and refreshing bathing place with three darkened sauna rooms, three small warm pools, and a large cold-water outdoor pool. After spending hours enjoying the sauna and pools, one could repair to a room with cots, where an attendant would come along to bundle one up with blankets. I've probably never had a more relaxing and refreshing nap than after my first sauna.

The word "sauna" refers both to a Finnish bathing tradition dating from ancient times and also to the building in which one bathes. The earliest type of sauna was a simple hole dug into a hillside around a rock post-and-lintel type of structure. Rocks were mounded inside the hole, and beneath them a fire was lit. A smokehole cut out of the hillside acted as a chimney. When the smoke cleared, the hole was plugged up, the bathers entered and doused the rocks with water; then they sweated and scrubbed themselves. When they'd had enough heat, they'd run out, jump in a lake or roll in the snow, and crawl back into the steamy cave. The log sauna, with a smokehole and an open firepit, evolved from this early hillside pit. The *savusauna*, or smoke sauna, got its name from the smoke-blackened inner walls and their smoky smell. A few purists in Finland still prefer the smoke sauna, but the more popular version today is the log sauna with a sod roof, masonry or iron stove, and a chimney.

The first sauna I built was up the road a half mile from our house, where we turned what had been a vegetable stand into a wood-fired sauna. But when I moved to the Nearings' old house in 1980, I knew that the island in the middle of the pond out back was the place where one day I'd build a log sauna. By the Spring of 1985, a friend, Steve Hanson, had girdled enough spruce trees to make a 10-foot-by-10-foot building. Girdling the trees means removing enough bark and layers of cambium to effectively keep the sap from rising in the tree, so that it dies and begins shrinking. The following Spring, Steve cut down the trees, and I peeled the logs and hauled them up to the building site.

On the island, we dug out an area 12 feet by 12 feet to a depth of 1 foot. We filled this with crushed rock and laid flat stones at the corners of a 10-foot square, which would act as a foundation. The finished sauna was planned to measure 10 feet by 10 feet outside and about 8½ feet square on the inside. Steve Hanson, a master with a chainsaw and a fine woodworker, did all the log work. In our case, that meant joining the logs with half-dovetailed notches to make tight, strong corners, which also created a traditional appearance that we liked. The first round of logs forming the base of the structure was cedar, which we chose because of its ability to resist rot; all additional wood was spruce. The bottom logs rested on the rock corners and were partially covered with gravel.

We intentionally left a 1-inch gap between the logs, and after attaching a metal lath between them on the inside and out, we filled the gap with fiberglass batting. Then

we used a 1:2:3 formula of cement, lime, and sand for the chinking mixture, which I applied with a mason's trowel. Another friend, Steve Cote, gave me an old sauna stove, which we mounted on the exterior of the building. This type of stove allows the fire to draw air from outside the building instead of through it. Also, it is loaded from outside, so wood does not need to be brought into the building. We set the stove into a cast-concrete frame next to the door.

I had seen sod roofs in Norway and thought that this traditional roof covering gave a

building a more "grounded" feeling. Plus, it was the most favored material for saunas in Finland. We supported the sod roof with 4-inch-by-8-inch purlins on 2-foot centers, decked over with 1-inch ship-lapped spruce boards. In the old days, layers of birchbark were used as a waterproof barrier between the roof sheathing and the sod. But on the recommendation of our friend Parker Waite, we covered the sheathing with three layers of Tyvek,™ a material which prevents water from passing into the sheathing but still allows water vapor to pass between the sauna and sod roof.

The best sod is said to come from a field that has a good growth of grasses, clover, and vetch, producing a dense root system. Since we had such a field, we had plenty of good sod. Over the Summer I kept a patch of it mowed, and in August I cut the sod into 1-foot squares that were 4 inches thick. Mark Dietrich pulled these up with a front-end loader on a tractor and put them in a pickup truck for transport to the bridge over to the island sauna. There, the sod was loaded into a wheelbarrow for the short trip to the sauna roof. We used two layers on the roof: The first went on upside down; the second layer grass side up. This arrangement discourages roots from growing into the roof and gives the top layer organic matter to live on.

Inside the sauna, we built three tiers of benches with a

16½-inch space between each level. The width of the lowest bench is 18 inches, the middle is 20 inches, and the top is 24 inches. All three benches run the length of the back wall, and the top bench turns 90 degrees to run part way along the east wall. As protection, the benches and ceiling were given a coating of linseed oil and turpentine mixed 1:1. On top of the gravel floor, we built slats with a ¼-inch gap between them.

The sauna has given us great pleasure; in fact, bathing has become a communal ritual. Several of our friends have now built their own saunas, and every Wednesday we get together at one of them for a bath followed by a potluck supper. When friends come to visit from far away, we always start off their stay with a sauna to wash away the cares and distance between us.

Maine in Summer has a surprising similarity with the tropics. The junglelike speed of growth in this part of the world has much to do with the extra length of the days as well as ideal growing conditions—evening dew, coastal fog, lots of Spring rain, and long, warm but not hot Summer days. The record high for the first day of Summer was 90 degrees set in 1963. The hillsides, which have a sparse layer of grass at the end of May, are luxuriant with wildflowers by July.

As the Summer weeks unfold, shasta daisies, delphiniums, veronicas, cosmos, calendula, foxglove, monkshood, and other flowers both wild and cultivated burst into bloom. The strong-colored zinnias, asters, dahlias, and black-eyed susans follow, and they are as brilliant as anything in a torrid climate, where petals have a tinge of blue to protect the flower from the sun's intensity. Maine's low-level light produces floral colors that seem luminescent.

It seems only natural to preserve this abundant flora, so during the Summer months, our wreath making is at its peak. As early as June, we begin harvesting flowers, cutting those we've raised in the garden and gathering others from the overgrown fields and roadsides.

The pond teems with life and the garden fairly bursts with it. By mid-July the beans, cucumbers, zucchini, and raspberries are ripe, and we double our preserving efforts in the kitchen. But August is the culinary month all mouths water for, when the blueberries, tomatoes, corn, and melons are ready to eat. Then too the winds are just right for sailing, and we plan picnics on the islands. New England's cuisine is famous, not for the complexity of its preparation but for its honest simplicity. The sweet corn barely needs butter or salt to be incredibly good. The potato is a work of art when sprinkled with fresh dill, and what does a lobster, crab, mussel, or clam need but some butter?

As August wanes, we play croquet on the lawn in the late afternoon when the shadows lengthen, already aware that another Summer spectacle will soon come to a close. The season is extra sweet because it is fleeting, and before we are ready to have Summer leave us, it does, taking the seasonal visitors with it. The long Labor Day weekend is a reminder that soon the birds will be going south and the leaves on the oak, ash, birch, and maple will give one final shout of color before the land is plunged once more into its customary dormant state. Then we will ask ourselves once more, "Where did the Summer go?"

*W*ild lupines bloom around the first day of Summer, their striking blue, pink, purple, and white flowers blanketing the hillside in front of the house (above), as if to take away any doubt we might have that Summer has come. A startled white-tailed deer happens through our field (right) before bolting for the woods.

*O*n the longest evening of the year, the sun sets around 9 P.M. (previous page). The huge waning moon, full only two nights ago, still casts a powerful glow, and we celebrate the Summer solstice—and the health of our crops, community, and earth—with friends.

The rugged rugosa roses are hardy plants that enjoy our salt air and easily survive our Winters. We cut them for wreaths when they are still tightly budded.

June 22

Last night we joined friends and neighbors to celebrate the Summer solstice, the turning point in the sun's journey when, after climbing higher and higher in the sky since last December 21st, the great luminary reaches its apex and retraces its steps down the heavenly path. The sun rose at 4:44 A.M. today and will set at 8:07 P.M., which means it won't really be dark until around 9:00. The huge waning moon, which was full two days ago, will cast a powerful glow.

Despite the auspicious conjunction of solstice and full moon, our celebration wasn't as dramatic as those of our ancient forebears. We had no bonfire, as they did in the old days throughout Europe; we didn't march cows through fires to protect them against the spells of witches and wizards, as they did in Brittany; we didn't cast toadstools into the flames to thwart the power of the trolls and other evil spirits that may inhabit the night, as they did in parts of Norway. Instead, we followed the one truly heated event of the evening, a visit to the sauna, with a dip in the pond and all the cider we could drink and some spirited dancing. We did top off the evening, however, with a ritual of our own: Holding hands, we performed a circle dance to the success of our crops and the health of our community and the earth.

June 24

The garden is coming alive with color. At the end of June we begin to pick various grasses and flowers to dry for the wreaths: the cloverlike, pale purple chive flowers, clouds of yarrow, winter rye, sweet fern—a luxuriant leathery green that grows along the roadside—and rugosa roses, picked when they are just barely out and still tightly furled, after the sun has burned off the dew. Monkshood, Siberian iris, bearded iris, and the first brilliant yellow and orange calendulas are starting to flower, and the dwarf dahlias are only a few days away. Sweetbriar's insistent pink already breaks up the short meadows, and nearer the pond tall meadow rue's starry white clusters draw whirls of moths and butterflies.

As if to mark the solstice, the lupines are in full bloom. Masses of their brilliant blue, pink, purple, and white flowers cover the hillside to the northwest of the house. We just heard on the radio that the "Lupine Lady," Hilda Hamlin, died this Spring at the age of one hundred. *Lupinus polyphyllus*, or wild lupine flowers, bloom from May to July in open, sunny woods from Maine to Florida.

The lupines we are familiar with are the indigenous ones, but the Russell lupines, named for the hybridizer George Russell of Yorkshire, England, were spread by Hilda, with the help of friends, over much of our coastline. Known as "Hilda Lupina," the former professor of English at Smith College spent every Summer since 1904 at Christmas Cove near Damariscotta, Maine. Early on, she began spreading lupine seeds, which she imported from her native England, and the results of her work can be seen in the fields and verges throughout Maine. This year we want to try to introduce them into the area around our newly extended pond. Their seeds can be gathered in August, before the pealike pods burst, and replanted immediately.

In early Summer, after the first spell of hot weather, Richard Bakeman drives over on his tractor to cut the hay.

July 1

Richard Bakeman, whose ancestors settled Cape Rosier in the 1790s, came to cut the hay, as he has done here for many years. Bearded, burly Richard is as reliable as the seasons and has become a guidepost to many fond and whimsical memories. We remember the time he found a trembling newborn fawn that was unaccountably orphaned, and he carried her up to us to hold and comfort. We recall the hornet nests he has run over and been stung by, and the year he got stuck crossing over the stream. He had his bug net with him this year, a good thing because he would need it up in back where the ground was still wet and the squadrons of blackflies were out in force.

Richard didn't waste any time getting going, and soon the pleasant fragrance of fresh-cut hay was in the air and the fields took on a neat, manicured look. After three hours on the tractor, Richard took a break. We ate ice cream in the kitchen and talked about the dangers of using these machines that have become invaluable to us. "They can be some nasty," he said. I recalled a neighbor of my brother in Chester, Vermont, who was killed when his tractor rolled over a steep hill and crushed him. Richard and I agreed that rotary tillers, on the other hand, seem tame machines but are deceptive. When Richard was repairing a tiller one day, he took it down back to see if it was running all right and put it into gear with the tiller engaged. Before he knew it, he was on the ground and the tiller had run over his leg. He rolls up his pant leg and shows me a 6-inch-long white scar just below the knee. Last Summer, when I was tilling up the new ground behind the newly extended pond, I was trying to till in as close as

Each year around the Fourth of July, we cut the hay in our fields (top left). The hay is allowed to dry for a couple of days, and then we rake it into windrows and piles, as Megan Thomas is doing here (top right). Lynn stands on the finished pile (middle right) before we pick it up with the truck, with the help of Michelle Gordon and George Tufts (bottom left). Andrea DeFrancesco rides atop the hay to keep the load from falling off (bottom right).

possible to a young spruce tree. All of a sudden, the tiller started climbing the tree, a sapling maybe three inches in diameter. The tree bent halfway to the ground. When I disengaged the tiller and put it in reverse, it jumped back and the tree snapped back, hitting me in the face and knocking me down. Meanwhile the tiller raced off toward the pond. Luckily, I was able to get to it just before it went into the water.

One July morning, this young red fox appeared just down the road from us. The fox somewhat resembles a small collie or coyote, but both lack its white-tipped tail.

The amount of hay we get from year to year varies with the moisture and soil fertility. This year there seemed to be considerably less hay than last, but there is still plenty for mulching the tomatoes, eggplants, peppers, brassicas (cabbage family members), and beans. We never mulch near the lettuce, for we have found that this tends to encourage slugs. We also use hay in the compost piles, and, later in the year, to bank up the house and protect from freezing those crops left in the ground.

We cut the hay on Saturday and that night a light rain fell. Sunday was sunny except for a rain shower in the afternoon. But we needed a solid day of sun to dry out the hay. If we were lucky, we could rake it into windrows, and in a couple of days it would be dry enough to pick up with the truck and mound up into a pile approximately twenty feet in diameter. Scott used to remind us to think of a doughnut when building the pile: to keep the center lower than the perimeter until the very end or the finished pile would be too steep.

We needed at least three people to do the work most efficiently: George (who worked with us a few days a week) and myself to pick up the hay with our forks and Michelle (who makes wreaths for us) up on the truck to help get it off our forks and load it so it doesn't fall off. At the haypile, I got up on the truck, and George and Michelle distributed the hay on the pile as I threw it to them. Around and around they went as if dancing, stomping it down, keeping the hay evenly spread out.

Making the haypile is thirst-producing work, in anticipation of which we freeze a few gallons of our sweet cider every Fall. It was an unusually hot day for coastal Maine, probably 90 degrees, and we took plenty of cider breaks. The deerflies buzzed around our heads. It was dusty, sweaty work, and we coughed and cursed, but of all the jobs we do here none feels more connected to the earth than gathering the hay.

Rhubarb Wine

◆

We have found wine- and cider-making to be a very simple and enjoyable hobby, in addition to being money-saving. (The biggest problem I've had is waiting for the wine to age.) This rhubarb is one of my favorites, but under no circumstances should you use any portion of the plant's leaves. They contain a toxin—oxalic acid—which is tasteless but poisonous.

The basic ingredients in all wine-making are a fruit or vegetable, sugar, an acid, wine yeast, and water; grapes and apples supply their own yeast. You will need: two 5-gallon containers, a large strainer, a 5-gallon carboy, an air lock, 6 feet of plastic hose, and a hydrometer (available through wine-making suppliers). All materials in the wine-making process must be kept absolutely clean to avoid contamination.

◆

15 pounds rhubarb stalks

10 pounds sugar

5 gallons boiling water

1 packet all-purpose wine yeast

2 tablespoons sugar

Juice of 5 large lemons

◆

1.   Begin with two 5-gallon crocks. Slice the rhubarb and divide it between the crocks. Stir into each crock about 1¼ pounds sugar and let them sit for several hours to help draw out the juice.

2.   Add the remaining sugar and pour the boiling water over the fruit.

3.   To get the yeast started, dissolve it in a quart jar filled with warm water and 2 tablespoons of sugar. Let it stand overnight.

4.   The next day, add the yeast mixture and the lemon juice to the crocks. Cover the crocks with cheesecloth and let the mash foam and ferment for 5 to 10 days, or until the frothing subsides. Strain the liquid through a fine mesh strainer, leaving behind the residue, and transfer it to a 5-gallon glass jar called a "carboy."

5.   From now on, the liquid must be kept free of oxygen. This is controlled by use of a rubber stopper and an air lock, a plastic device containing water which allows carbon dioxide (the by-product of fermenting sugar and yeast) to escape while preventing oxygen from reaching the future wine. At first the water in the air lock will bubble furiously, sometimes so much so that some liquid will spill over. Watch the carboy carefully for the first few days.

6.   After about two weeks, much of the sediment will have settled at the bottom of the carboy. Using a plastic hose, siphon off the liquid, leaving behind the sediment at the bottom. Discard the sediment, clean the carboy, pour the wine back in, and air lock again.

7.   Let the wine sit for about 6 to 8 weeks. To determine whether it is ready to be bottled, take a reading with a hydrometer to see if all the sugar and yeast have been converted. A reading of 1.000 means it is ready to be bottled. (The hydrometer measures the specific gravity of a liquid. Water measures 1.000. Any liquid thicker than water will have a reading higher than 1.000. We start rhubarb wine with a reading of 1.085, which will give us a finished wine with 10 percent alcohol content.)

8.   Bottle the wine.

Yield: About 5 gallons

On the Fourth of July, most of the residents of our small town of Harborside march while the rest of the townsfolk look on. Leading the parade, here in front of John Howard's house (top left), were from left John Howard, Dick Brownell, Dick Klain, his son, and his granddaughter. All around the area and across the U.S.A., there are parades on this day, but ours was outstanding, if only for our very original wardrobe (this page and opposite).

July 5

We are a few weeks into Summer, and so far it has been a tough year for growing vegetables. There has been too much rain, not enough sun, and more of every bug than ever. At this time of year, we monitor the plants every day for bugs. Rarely and only as a last resort do we spray or dust the plants with insecticides. We try to live with the cutworms, spit bugs, leaf hoppers, and tarnished plant bugs, and we are able to fight flea beetles and cucumber beetles with Rotenone, a biological insecticide made from the root of the South American derris plant. This plant-derived insecticide has proven to be harmless to warm-blooded animals but kills many kinds of insects, including certain external animal parasites. It has little residual effect, but the period of protection it offers is short, so we have to spray regularly.

Blackflies, mosquitoes, and deerflies abound this year, forcing us to wear head nets and use a lot of bug dope, which I believe gives me headaches. However, switching from the commercial brands to an herbal variety containing pennyroyal oil has kept the bugs and the headaches at bay.

Mosquitoes have been around for fifty million years. They inhabit almost every kind of land surface, but half of the 2,700 species of mosquito stay in the rainforests, which may yet help preserve these most valuable forests from humanity's intrusion. The female finds her way to humans by sensing perspiration and higher skin temperatures. Italian folk wisdom has it that sleeping with a pig in the bedroom protects against malaria, presumably because the mosquitoes will prefer the pig's higher body temperature. Our well-screened house precludes our having to sleep with a pig.

July 8

This morning, as well as for the last five, the first thing I smelled on entering the kitchen was the sweet aroma of rhubarb wine in its early stages of fermentation. It will be about another six weeks before it is ready for bottling. Just outside the window, next to the flower box, I was thrilled to hear the unmistakable sound of a ruby-throated hummingbird, the only hummingbird of the 320 species of *Trochilidae* to visit us in the northeast. She was just two inches away from me, sipping nectar from some delphiniums with her long beak, ruby throat, and bright green iridescent plumage clearly visible. Hummingbirds are the only

birds known to fly backwards, and like swifts, they do not perch while feeding. Since they appear to be especially attracted to red flowers, we plant scarlet runner beans in pots near the house every year.

Given how harsh our climate is here on the Maine coast, the number of flowers that thrive, sometimes with minimal care, is amazing. Our campanulas, cosmos, calendula, dahlias, *Salvia hormonium*, roses, and zinnias are all in bloom. For over a month we have been enjoying columbine and *Salvia praetensis*—a perennial that seems to survive the worst of winters. It has beautiful, deep blue, claw-shaped flowers on long spikes. Delphiniums are at their peak, and we are beginning to supply local restaurants and inns with fresh flowers from the garden. My mother grew them, and as a child, I remember thinking that they must be the perfect blue. I still think so. Because we live on the coast and are subject to high winds, we've planted the variety "Dwarf Blue Fountains," which grow only 4 feet high, instead of 6 feet. They come in a wonderful range of colors, from pure white to light and dark blue, some with contrasting centers called "bees," because they appear to have a bee-seeking pollen in each bloom. Delphiniums are one of our rewards for living in this varied climate where winter temperatures can reach 30 degrees below zero. They are hardy perennials that require only minimum protection: We just spread wood ash over their roots and cover them with a layer of spruce boughs; every three to four years they need to be dug up and divided.

Dame's rocket *(Hesperis matronalis)* has been in bloom for over a month. The Latin *Hesperis* refers to evening, and it is at this time of day that the flower is at its most fragrant. I have been on a quest to naturalize this plant, so far without great success. I did find some white ones growing wild, dug them up, and transplanted them into our gardens, where I'm hoping they will produce seed.

Mary Stackhouse, who owned our farm before the Nearings, from 1946 to 1951, planted dozens of white shrub roses and monkshood, both of which are still thriving after over forty winters. Monkshood is in the delphinium family—*Ranunculaceae*—and is a wonderfully long-lasting cut flower. The Latinate name, Aconite, is the English form of its Greek name, *Lycotonum*, or wolf's bane, which derives from the ancient lore that arrows or bait soaked in its juice would kill wolves. In the Middle Ages, it became known as monkshood or "auld wife's huid" because of its helmet- or hood-shaped flowers. In 1981, a fellow from

Monkshood (above), planted back in the 1940s by Mary Stackhouse outside the walled garden, continues to thrive in our rugged climate.

Looking out to the fields, Pistachio enjoys the early Summer flower garden directly in front of the house (opposite).

Shasta daisies, monkshood, delphinium, and Salvia hormonium *are some of the flowers we begin selling to restaurants and inns in early Summer (above).*

Morning glories, Ipomoea purpurea, *which grow in pots alongside the barn, up archways, and around windows, provide beautiful blue and purple blooms from early Summer into October (right).*

Columbines, herbaceous perennials of great beauty be-
longing to the buttercup family *(above)*, are among the
first flowers we cut and dry for wreaths.

Peonies, Festivea maxima *(left)*, are a favorite
early flowering perennial.

England, Trevor Field, happened by our farm on his bicycle; he liked it here and stayed a month. His favorite flower, it turned out, was the dark blue "auld wife's huid." He had a wonderful way of pronouncing it, and I've tried and tried to imitate it, but to no avail.

Maude Grieve tells us in *A Modern Herbal*: "Theophastis like Pliny derived the name from Aconoe, the supposed place of its origin. Napellus, the variety we have, signifies a little turnip, an allusion to the shape of the roots." Ms. Grieve tells us further that monkshood is much used in homeopathic medicine, especially for such ailments as flu which appear suddenly. Because of its very poisonous nature, however, all medicines obtained from monkshood come under Table I of the Poison Schedule:

> The official tincture taken internally diminishes the rate and force of the pulse in the early stages of fevers and slight local inflammation, it relieves pain of neuralgia, pleurisy and aneurysm. It is the root which contains the strongest poison. $\frac{1}{50}$ grain of aconite will kill a sparrow in five minutes. So acrid is the poison that the juice applied to a wounded finger affects the whole system, not only causing pain in the limbs but a sense of suffocation and syncope. In 1524 and 1526 it is recorded that two criminals to whom the root was given as an experiment quickly died.

July 10

Late this afternoon Lynn and I were working in the walled garden when one of our cats, Gusto, decided it was time to have her kittens. Soothing her as she rolled that unmistakable low yowl from the depths of her sagging belly, we brought her into the barn and fixed up a box on a shelf about four feet above the ground. She rejected this and clambered up to the next shelf into an old box still filled with some of last year's hydrangea. In minutes, she had given birth to the first of four kittens. By carefully cutting out part of the side of the box, we were able to see her licking the orange fur of a tiny, plump baby. Two of the kittens didn't make it, perhaps because their mother was less than a year old and didn't have enough milk to feed them. But for the next two months the surviving twins, Wheezo and Gaspacho, became the center of everyone's attention.

The beach yields many treasures, including the driftwood we use for the multitude of whimsical scarecrows set up around the farm. It is thought that scarecrows originated in Greece and Japan around the same time—at least 2,000 years ago—both as sentinels to ward off birds and evil spirits and as fertility symbols.

On July 10, Gusto gave birth to twins, Wheezo and Gaspacho, as we later named them. At birth, they were hardly larger than field mice, but they grew and grew, providing us with endless fascination.

A week after the birth, Lynn was sitting under the lilac tree when Gusto appeared with one of the kittens, so new its eyes were still closed, hanging from her jaws by the nape of its neck. She deposited this one at Lynn's feet and went to get the other—she was so proud of her fine job of mothering. It would be another five days before the kittens would open their eyes, but she would bring them out and show them to us almost every day and return them to their safe nest after about a half hour. Lynn and I chuckled at her newfound pride, but admitted to one another that our own accomplishments were quite humble compared to Gusto's work this season.

July 15

We scythed the comfrey today and added the leaves to the compost piles. This is a good time to dig up some of the roots to make comfrey salve. Comfrey, *Symphytum officinale*, is a native of Asia and has been used by herbalists to cure a wide range of ills for over two thousand years. In 400 B.C., Herodotus recommended comfrey compresses to stop the flow of blood; the Romans carried comfrey among their curative agents when they conquered Europe; it is found on monastery lists and in Saxon leechbooks dated around A.D. 1000; in the fourteenth century, comfrey was recommended as a cure for sore throat and whooping cough and as a poultice for bruises and open wounds. Comfrey's folk name, knitbone, came from its use in healing broken bones.

Because of its very high component of usable potash, Scott Nearing grew a lot of comfrey to use in building compost piles, where it is best combined with seaweed, manure, kitchen garbage, and other green matter. We sometimes make a concentrated fertilizer tea of comfrey by filling a barrel a quarter full of fresh-cut leaves and three-quarters full of water. After a week or two, when the liquid is a dark green, it can be fed directly to the plants as a quick dose of potassium. (A note of caution: There is a still unresolved controversy about the safety of eating comfrey, because it contains a pyrrolizidine alkaloid.)

Comfrey is a tenacious plant and is all but impossible to dig up; if any portion of the long taproot and subsidiary roots is left behind, it will give birth to new plants, so it should only be planted away from other plants, where it won't need to be moved.

COMFREY SALVE

For this salve I combine comfrey leaves with leaves of *Plantago major*—the common plantain that grows by our roadsides and is a stubborn weed on garden lawns. I use the salve to heal the skin, as a preventive against dry skin, or on my face after shaving.

1 cup grated comfrey root

1 cup finely chopped plantain leaves

2 quarts olive oil

4 cups grated beeswax (see Note)

1. Place the grated comfrey root in a quart jar. Place the chopped plantain leaves in a second quart jar. Fill both jars to the top with olive oil. Let the jars stand out of direct sunlight for 6 weeks.

2. Strain contents of each jar through cheesecloth into a large saucepan. Add grated beeswax and heat very slowly, stirring constantly, until the wax is melted. Pour the mixture into clean glass jars—such as mustard or jam jars—and cool. The salve should be creamy but solid.

Yield: About 12 small jars

Note: Beekeepers and some health food stores can supply beeswax.

HERB VINEGAR

◆

Herb vinegars are both easy to make and a great way to store up the taste of summer herbs. We use the vinegars in salads and soups.

Fill clean, clear or pale-green wine bottles with clear white distilled or white wine vinegar. Add sprigs of favorite herbs such as tarragon, basil, dill, or thyme—but don't mix the herbs. We like garlic a lot and add a chopped-up clove to each bottle. In the past, I have added a few raspberries to each bottle for color and flavor, but this year I tried using a small amount of red wine vinegar to achieve a pleasant pale pink color. Cap the bottles with corks and set aside for a few weeks to allow flavors to mingle.

July 20

Sitting in my chair in the kitchen near the window, I noticed the heavy, sweet scent of the petunias in the window box filling the air. I had read that the reason some plants give off more perfume at night is to attract night-flying moths for pollination; I'm always amazed at nature's creative ways.

The herbs and flowers in the small 4-foot-by-12-foot kitchen garden right outside our mudroom door are in full Summer bloom. Geranium, lobelia, nasturtiums, basil, and thyme spill out of clay pots, and morning glories and scarlet runner beans climb all over the walls of the house and barn. In the stone-edged garden itself, kitchen herbs—tarragon, parsley, oregano, coriander, dill, spearmint, peppermint, catnip, and sweet cicely (*Myrrhis odorata*, a perennial herb of the carrot family grown for its aromatic fernlike foliage)—flourish amid brilliant orange and yellow calendula flowers. Calendula leaves have a pungent, pleasing taste and are often found in Indian cooking, while the flowers are used medicinally as a tincture or an ointment for treating cuts, burns, and sprains.

Some of our favorite flowers are reserved for this spot by the back door: petunias, violas, anthemis, columbine, zinnias, *Salvia hormonium*, lobelia, and a newly planted climbing rose. In the walled garden the delphinium that we use both in the wreaths and for cut flowers has finished blooming, and we are scything down the plants. If we have a long, mild Fall we will get a second cutting of delphiniums sometime in October. Larkspur, in the same family as delphinium, is both our favorite wreath flower and the flower we find the most difficult to grow because of its aversion to dampness. This year the larkspur struggled, but it appears we will harvest a fair amount. Sea lavender, which acts as a base on most of the wreaths because of its wonderful light color and airy texture, is ready to be harvested from one of the islands close to our house. Vegetables in the walled garden we are now harvesting regularly are zucchini, cucumbers, peas, lettuce, arugula, radishes, beans, swiss chard, beets, carrots, basil, dill, and parsley.

July 24

We are now experiencing the full heat of Summer. Today the temperature reached the high 80s, and the gardens felt the lack of moisture. It seemed we might reach 90 degrees, the record temperature for this date set in 1963. The

*F*lower boxes are full of petunias on the west side of the house. In mid-July, the petunias stand over two feet high and are still growing (above). We love the effect of looking from inside the house out through a small jungle of these fragrant purple, pink, and white blossoms.

*G*usto guards the archway and kitchen garden (left) where we grow many of our favorite herbs: parsley, oregano, basil, thyme, sage, coriander, hyssop, and giant hyssop (Agastache).

*O*ur perennial border is at its peak in early to mid-July when the masses of foxgloves and delphiniums are in bloom. Phlox, rambling roses, and clematis have been interplanted along with rudbeckias, hollyhocks, monkshood, globe thistle, and sea holly (overleaf).

DILLY BEANS

◆

This recipe is a great way to use all those beans which seem to ripen at once, and it's a treat to pull a jar out of the root cellar in the Fall, Winter, and Spring. The beans are crunchy to the bite and really pucker your mouth up. We like them with just about everything from tuna sandwiches to leek soup.

◆

¾ pounds fresh green beans

2 cups cider vinegar

1 cup water

½ teaspoon pickling salt

Several sprigs fresh dill (about 10)

2 cloves garlic, chopped

◆

1. Trim the beans, then steam them 2 to 4 minutes, until just crisp-tender. Drain them, then thoroughly rinse them under cold water. Tightly pack the beans into two sterilized 1-quart jars.

2. In a 2- or 3-quart nonreactive (nonaluminum) saucepan, bring the vinegar, water, and salt to a boil. Pour the boiling mixture over the beans, then divide the dill and garlic between the jars. Green beans are a low-acid vegetable and must be canned carefully according to manufacturer's directions. Seal.

3. Wait two weeks before opening.

Yield: 2 quarts

By mid-July our vegetable harvest is at its peak. Here, the sweet, young carrots are washed and ready for market (top). The color and taste of rhubarb chard (above) make it a favorite salad ingredient.

grass is turning brown, the pond level is dropping, and the young lettuce transplants are wilting. Once they are established in the garden, we try not to water the plants so as to encourage them to grow stronger, deeper roots. But because of the drought, we reluctantly watered the lettuce, winter carrots, celery, and leeks today. Until this week we had only half an inch of rain in July, and many of our crops, such as potatoes, need closer to an inch a week.

We are in the middle of a Bermuda high pressure system that will probably last for several days. Ozone levels are expected to reach "unhealthful levels." I called the National Weather Service and discovered that this particular ozone is at ground level, rather than up in the stratosphere, and is formed by hydrocarbons reacting with sunlight, the O_2 changing to O_3. The hydrocarbons are released by cars; power plants that burn coal, oil, or gas; and other heavy industrial users of fossil fuels from Massachusetts and New York. A neighbor, who now lives mostly in Vermont, summed up our community's reaction: "I'm horrified to think we have to put up with New York City's pollution."

High ozone levels have been a problem for us for the last few Summers and are dangerous, not just for the elderly and those with respiratory disease, but for anyone. Authorities recommend that anyone doing strenuous exercise such as jogging do so in the morning before the levels get too high. According to a recent article in *Organic Gardening* magazine, yellow, brown, or purple spots on older leaves of beans, Concord grapes, or morning glories could indicate ozone pollution. High ozone levels age plants prematurely, shorten their growing season, and cause them to drop leaves.

Wild raspberries have come out near the woods and along the roadsides. Every time I go down to collect our mail I also walk over to Helen Nearing's mailbox, where just to the waterside, the hill falls steeply off. There, the berries grow plentifully, not enough to make pies or jam, but plenty to eat on the spot. Here on the coast our supply of wild foods is so bountiful. One could survive well on the mushrooms, rosehips, blueberries, various edible greens like orach (a relative of spinach), sea rocket, tangy sheep sorrel, glasswort, and, of course, the plentiful fresh mussels and clams, lobsters, crabs, and mackerel.

August 4

Officially, we are halfway through Summer. Today we began to harvest the high-bush blueberries. The cherry tomatoes, a variety called "Sweet 100s," are ripe and make a nice treat in salads, but the regular tomatoes need a few more sunny days to ripen. The first harvesting of each crop is always cause for celebration; each time we feel as if it's the first time we've ever had a tomato or a blueberry. August is the month we all wait for, the month of most intense heat, the month when our prized vegetables ripen—corn, tomatoes, peppers, eggplant, and melons. And yet we are aware that, when this time of plenty does at last arrive, we are also not far from the end of Summer, when the nights will become perceptively cooler and the days shorter.

By mid-July, the neighbor's kids, Plumi and Gigi, and their friends spend hours in the pond, poling the raft and jumping and knocking each other off it (above). Ollie runs off the sauna island (opposite). The echoes of their laughter often draw us out of the gardens and fields to make our own refreshing dash into the water.

Of course, even in the heat of Summer we prepare for the rest of the year. With an eye out for the cold weather to come, we have filled our woodshed. It holds about five cords of wood (a cord of wood is 128 cubic feet and is commonly measured as a pile 4 feet wide, 4 feet high, and 8 feet long), all of which we'll need come Winter. Scott Nearing used to say "dry wood under cover is better than money in the bank," and if you've ever lived through Winter in Maine, you'll know he was right.

Nature follows its own routine, and I've found that it is important to know which jobs can be put off on the farm. This knowledge comes with understanding the crops, the weather, and ourselves and developing a rhythm that allows for a fairly even flow of work. Otherwise, one can get totally overwhelmed, as I often was in my early years here.

Record keeping is an essential but often neglected part of learning to be a gardener. It is necessary to keep notes on weather conditions, planting dates, varieties of seeds that worked and those that didn't, dates and amounts of harvest, and insect problems and how they were dealt with. In addition, one must map out what is planted and where, list the crops to be succession-planted and the types of supplements to be added to the soil, and make plans for new varieties to try next year. The better our records, the easier it is not to repeat mistakes and to improve our gardens.

August 6

Yesterday, I went fishing with Manu Semann, a sixteen-year-old German boy who is staying with us. The fog was thick enough to cut with a knife, and we had to stick very close to the shore, using the motor and no sails on our 18-foot

Once we catch our first mackerel of the season—they usually arrive in mid-July—we get fish fever. Here, in early August, Manu and I carry the coracle down to the water (above) and then paddle it (right) to the sailboat, which we take out fishing.

sailboat as we trolled for mackerel. Suddenly Manu yelled, "Stop! Stop! I have fish!" I put the motor into neutral, he hauled in his line, and sure enough, he had four mackerel, all putting up quite a fight. Manu managed to haul in these beautiful fish, with their shimmering green and blue backs and white bellies. The Atlantic mackerel, *Scomber scombrus*, are found from Labrador to Cape Hatteras and generally arrive in Maine in mid-July, chasing the herring that flourish here then; they leave for warmer waters in early September. Along with mackerel come schools of bluefish, but I have yet to catch any.

Once we catch the mackerel, we get fish fever. They can be as big as 22 inches and 3 pounds, though the largest of yesterday's catch was 17 inches and 2 pounds. We enjoy them most cooked over an open fire, which is what we did last night. We split the mackerel lengthwise to release some of the oil during cooking. Lemon-dill dressing made the mackerel even more delicious. A light rain began to fall, so we retreated into the house with the cooked mackerel, and Lynn, Manu, and I sat down to a meal that also included parsley and potatoes, a salad of greens, cucumbers, and carrots from the garden, some of last year's rhubarb wine, and fresh blueberry pie. Ah, sweet Summertime.

Miso obviously has an opinion about—or at least a desire for—Manu's catch of the day. Later, we cook the fish our favorite way—grilled over hot coals.

MANU'S LEMON DILL DRESSING

◆

3 lemons

½ cup white wine or white distilled vinegar

2 tablespoons French mustard such as Dijon

2 tablespoons sugar

½ teaspoon salt

½ cup olive oil

¼ cup water

½ cup finely chopped fresh dill

◆

Grate the zest of 1½ lemons and and set aside. Squeeze juice from all the lemons. Combine the zest and juice in a small bowl with the vinegar, mustard, sugar, and salt. Whisk in the oil and then the water. Stir in the dill. (This dressing can also be made in a blender.)

Yield: 2 cups

Penobscot Bay appears in the background of this blueberry field in the nearby town of Sedgewick (top left). The wild blueberry harvest there is in full gear in mid-August. "Rakers," often migrant workers, use a multi-tined steel rake (above) to do their arduous work; note the correct position of the raker in the background (top). After the rakers dump the berries into a bucket, winnowing machines (left) separate the leaves from the berries.

August 10

The wild blueberry harvest is in full swing here in Hancock County and further up the coast in Washington County. Known as lowbush blueberries, *Vaccinium angustifolium* grow 6 to 18 inches high on well-drained and acidic soils. The blueberry barrens, as they are called here in Maine, are generally burned or flail-mowed for pruning and weed control every second year in the Fall or early Spring. This year due to the severe Winter, lack of snow cover, and the very wet Spring, the crop will be about 10 percent below normal, yielding about 26 million pounds. This represents about half of the total U.S. production.

The blueberry fields are laid out with strings in very long strips 10 to 12 feet wide. The workers who collect the berries are called "rakers," after the instrument they use in the harvest. Rakers are assigned to specific long strips to ensure that the entire field gets picked. The rake they use is a steel instrument with a short, inverted handle and a flat, high-sided scoop tipped with thin tines. The hours are long and the work is backbreaking. The raker, bending, pushes the rake forward and into the plants, then pulls up in a sweeping motion. As the tines strip the berries from the bushes, they roll into the reservoir at the back of the scoop. Rakers use 5-gallon buckets to collect the berries, which come along with stems and leaves. Winnowing machines then separate the berries from the chaff.

Harvesting in this area is often done by migrant farm workers, including local Penobscot Indians and Micmac Indians from Nova Scotia. They are paid by the pound or the box; this year the price varied from 10¢ to 20¢ a pound, or $2.50 to $5.00 a box. Although 99 percent of the berries are frozen immediately, 15 percent are later repacked in cans. The biggest buyers of frozen berries are large bakeries, but a local winery is now making a fine wine from fresh ones.

August 11

We have had a lot of morning fog lately, but it is supposed to burn off at last. The Maine coast has some of the most spectacular fogs in the world, caused by the confluence of the warm Gulf Stream and the icy Labrador Current somewhere offshore. The fogs drift in from the Bay of Fundy or the North Atlantic. The farther "Down East" you go, the more likely you are to find yourself fogbound; we

BLUEBERRY WINE

Berry wines can be made following the basic steps outlined in the recipe for Rhubarb Wine.

♦

5 gallons blueberries

10 pounds sugar

4 gallons water

Juice of 10 lemons

1 package all-purpose wine yeast

2 tablespoons sugar

♦

1. Place the blueberries in a large pot over high heat. Stirring constantly, bring to a simmer, and cook until the berries burst.

2. Transfer the berries to a large crock and add the sugar, water, and lemon juice.

3. Dissolve the packet of yeast in a quart of warm water and 2 tablespoons sugar and set aside. The next day, add this liquid to the berry mixture. Cover the crock with cheesecloth.

4. Let the mixture stand for about 2 weeks, or until the frothing subsides. Strain it into a 5-gallon carboy and air lock.

5. Proceed as for directions in Rhubarb Wine recipe (see page 62).

Yield: About 5 gallons

*By mid-August the garden yields a daily bounty
of vegetables, including lettuce, potatoes, and green
beans (above).*

*The yards are overflowing with flowers by mid-Summer.
Miso surveys the new perennial garden from the stone
wall (opposite).*

are about halfway between Kittery and Eastport and suffer our fair share. The ocean temperature today was in the low 60s and visibility at or near zero.

Scott Nearing once told me that in the Summer of 1969, there were only three days of sun in July, making gardening all but impossible. That foggy year produced a monstrous invasion of slugs, leaving behind slimy, viscous trails and devastating young plants beyond recovery. This Summer we had less of a slug problem than usual, in part because of the depth of last Winter's severe frost and the long dry period in early Summer. Nevertheless, we grow all our lettuce seedlings on scaffolding four feet above ground level so as not to tempt the slimy gastropods. Friends from the Pacific northwest tell us we're lucky not to have to deal with the 5-inch-long banana slugs they encounter.

Fog or not, it was time to bail the rainwater out of the sailboat. So down at the shore in a fog thick as pea soup, I raised the coracle, a tiny, canvas-covered, willow-framed boat, over my head and carried it down to the water, looking like some giant turtle as I slipped and slid in high boots over the rockweed. These rocks were so slick that I had to intentionally slide down, looking for barnacles to get a better grip. It was nearly high tide, so I didn't have to carry the coracle far. Paddling it out to the sailboat, I was struck by the stillness of the silence, the black-green spruce trees, the grayness all around me fading into deeper grayness.

The whoosh of a seagull's wings filled the heavy air. A pair of double crested cormorants—huge black birds the size of geese—were outlined against the fog. The cormorant—*Phalacromat auritus*—derives its English name from French through the Latin name *corvus marinus*, meaning sea crow. These birds often use the same resting spots as sea gulls—friends, I guess, in the game of survival. We often see them heading to their nests of seaweed on the islands, flying low, perhaps two feet over the water, beating their huge wings. The fog was a comfort this Sunday morning; it was good to appreciate the marginal view, a closer look at our great coastline.

Back on shore a gray squirrel chattered nervously up in a fir tree, probably warning its young of cats on the prowl. Walking back up the driveway to the house, I noticed that the wild carrot, or Queen Anne's lace, was in full bloom in the lower field and here and there some early goldenrod bloomed. But black-eyed susans were dropping petals, and the clusters of buttercups didn't seem as bright and thick as a week ago. The days were getting shorter.

CREATING DRIED-FLOWER WREATHS

Dried flowers have a delicate beauty and a wonderful palette and texture all their own. We hang hundreds of bunches of flowers from the ceiling of the wreath workshop in the barn. Upon entering, people look up and are overtaken by the abundant colors, which look as if they had been painted by an impressionist. Rows of blues and purples of statice, delphinium, and larkspur give way to the pinks, apricots, yellows, beiges, and whites of the chives, tansy, black-eyed susans, buttercups, yarrow, and pearly everlasting. During the late Summer and early Fall—wreath-making season—the floor of our work-

shop gets covered with all the flower petals and straw clippings.

We grow the flowers for our wreaths in our upper garden, an area of about a quarter acre to the northeast of the house. Here we planted rows 80 feet long and 3 feet wide of *Artemesia ludoviciana*, statice, *Helichrysum*, *Nigella* or love-in-a-mist, *Celosia*, *Amobium*, globe amaranth, larkspur, *Salvia hormonium*, and *Salvia victoria*. I also started *Gypsophelia paniculata* or baby's breath, *Santolina*, German statice, *Stachys lanata* or lamb's ears, *Agastache* or hyssop, sage, and pink yarrow. From friends I obtained cuttings of various artemesias, which add a wonderful pale silver green to the wreaths; marjoram, which dries to a fine deep purple; and many chive plants. We have recently expanded that garden so that we can rotate the annuals each year, putting in a cover crop for a few years to restore the soil's fertility.

Other abundant sources of flowers, which actually yield much of our dried-flower harvest, are overgrown fields and roadsides. We find various grasses; rabbit's-foot clover;

white yarrow; vetch, with its small lavender-like flowers and pale green foliage; sweet fern (a fine-smelling, dark green, leafy plant once used by the Native Americans for tea); goldenrod; tansy; and the valuable sea lavender with its airy, fresh feeling. In the Fall we gather spruce cones, rosehips, birchbark, barberry, milkweed, and iris seed pods, which lend a wintry quality to the wreaths.

The first flowers for our wreaths are the rugosa roses which we begin picking in early June from the large clump near the house. We cut them when still in a tight bud and dry them upstairs in the barn on large screens. The chive flowers bloom then too. We gather these in bunches, held together with rubber bands. Along with most of the other flowers for the wreaths, these are hung upside down from the rafters of the barn.

The best dried flowers are those picked when the weather is dry and the morning dew has burned off the blooms. Flowers should be dried away from direct sunlight, which fades their color. Strip the leaves from the lower part of each stem, and bunch them together with a

rubber band. Do not crowd too many flowers together; air should be able to circulate around them. Hang the flowers from a nail or along a cord until they feel dry and crisp. It usually takes between five and ten days for the flowers to dry, depending mostly on the weather conditions. Damp foggy days are the bane of wreath flowers and drying. Some years we have lost all the larkspur and much of the statice, two valuable wreath plants that are most vulnerable to dampness.

For our wreath-making we use the following materials: a wreath ring, a backing, flowers, and wire to connect the flowers and backing to the ring. You can buy crimped wreath rings from a florist supply, or rings can be made of willow or even coat hangers. We use three basic sizes: 3½-inch, 5-inch, and 8-inch diameters.

Begin a wreath by wiring a backing to the ring. For this we use #24 painted green spool wire, also available from a florist supply. We've found that dried hay makes a very suitable backing material. Most of our wreaths have a sea lavender base over which we weave the various dried flowers, seed pods, and grasses. Before starting to make the wreath, we decide which flowers are to be included and what overall tone the wreath will have, such as pink, apricot, blue, or purple.

Before attaching the flowers to the wreath, we form clusters of varied flowers in the hand and wire each cluster to the backing. The next cluster is wired in behind the last, thereby hiding the wire and stems. We continue adding groups of flowers until the entire wreath is full. If it is done properly, we cannot tell where we started or ended. But sometimes there will be gaps in the wreath where we need to add a few more flowers. We do this using a 3-inch florist's pick, which comes with wire attached to it.

When the wreath is finished, we form a wire loop at the back. We hang it up, stand back, and trim off any flowers that are out of place or add a few more as needed. If wreaths are hung inside out of direct sunlight, they should last several years. We recommend misting with water twice a year.

August 19

We have had 1½ inches of rain in the past week. A whopping ⁷⁄₁₀ inch pelted us in an hour during one of those wild Summer storms when all of a sudden the sky goes nearly black and the air gets very still, and then the wind blows and the downpour begins. This new moisture gives the mushrooms a chance to grow, so later I slipped into the woods and headed for a place where I had gathered chanterelles in previous years. Sure enough, there they were; I collected a bagful, some of which I planned to have for dinner.

I first discovered the chanterelle and other mushrooms in a beautiful beech forest above a river in Germany in the late 1960s. At first, all mushrooms just looked like a bunch of multicolored toadstools to me. However, with the help of a friend and later two field guides, I became able to identify many fungi.

Mushrooms differ from green plants in that they have no chlorophyll and so cannot obtain food from that inorganic source—sunlight. Instead, they can only destroy or change compounds that have already been built. Mushrooms are either terrestrial, that is, growing in the humus or soil, or lignicolous, that is, living on wood. The deadwood in the forest is reduced to humus by the activity of the fungi. After the mushroom plant has taken everything it can use from a log, it dies. In the meantime, it has produced a fruit—the mushroom—which in turn produces innumerable small bodies (spores) that are discharged and carried away by air currents. The spores start to grow once they land in a favorable spot.

The chanterelle, *Cantharellus cibarius*, is more or less egg-yolk yellow over its entire body. It is fragrant when both fresh and dried, smelling somewhat like fresh apricots; it has a smooth cap with wavy to lobed margins and long, descending (decurrent) gills that are often forked and have obtuse edges, at least when young. It grows in particular under oaks and conifers. The name is derived from the French diminutive of the Greek *kantharos* (cup). Chanterelles are best collected in August and September in the east and from September to February in the west. Found throughout North America, they keep well for a few days and can also be dried successfully. I clean them with a mushroom brush, trim off their dirty stems, and then dry them in the sun. The chanterelle is listed in mushroom hunters' guides as edible and choice, a gourmet species.

Our field guide cautions us to compare it carefully with the poisonous *Clitocybe illudens*, the so-called jack-o'-lantern fungus. This fungus seems to grow

My favorite chanterelles (opposite) and the Agaricus campestris *(above) are but two of the many edible mushrooms that grow in our area. Mushrooms should not be washed, but rather brushed free of needles, leaves, and dirt before cooking. We prefer to sauté the mushrooms in butter and serve them over rice or in omelettes, but since so many edible mushrooms look very much like poisonous ones, it's not wise to eat any of them until you have absolutely confirmed what you have.*

The perennial purple coneflowers are especially attractive to butterflies.

in longer clusters than the chanterelle, and its gills are much sharper. Another clue is that when the jack-o'-lantern is collected in its actively growing condition and taken into a dark room, its luminous gills give off an eerie green glow.

We like to slowly sauté freshly picked chanterelles in butter in a large iron skillet over a low flame. They are cooked until tender and served over rice with fresh tomato and basil salad; we can't get enough of them. Around this time of Summer we should also be finding coral mushrooms, *Clavaria cinerea*, up in the damp woods behind the house. *Boletus edulis*, or Steinpilz, will also be turning up. This fine-tasting mushroom is unpredictable, sometimes growing abundantly in what seems to be a dry season, and because of this collectors are not prone to give away information as to where this species can be found.

August 27

The sound of crickets fills the air until I think the ringing is in my ears. But no, it is *Gryllus assimilis*. The males sing by rubbing their wings, perhaps with the purpose of defying other males. It is a quiet, sunny Sunday, and sitting by the pond reading *The New York Times*, I luxuriate in the gentle warmth and pace of late Summer. The sun has become more precious as it has lost its earlier strength; now, I no longer sit with my back to it. I watch as amber-winged dragonflies hover and dart about the pond eating insects. The cats laze about in the shade dreaming of frogs' legs and grilled mackerel. Ospreys circle high in the sky.

We have finished planting food crops from seed this year, but there is still lettuce to transplant, spinach to thin, and the greenhouse to fill with hardy escarole, bok choy, kale, and spinach. Winter rye will be planted as a cover crop over all the gardens once we harvest the crops after the first of September. The cucumbers, tomatoes, peppers, and eggplants are being harvested now. The leaves on the birch trees are turning yellow and hanging limp, as if to say, "We're tired and ready to drop." These days, we look for ripening apple trees along the roadsides where we can gather apples for cider in early October.

The weather is beginning to turn clear and cool, especially at night, and the bird migration is beginning as well. The flickers that we last saw in May on their way north have returned. These beautiful birds are woodpeckers, of the family *Picidae* and subspecies *Colaptes auratus*. Their brown backs, yellow-tipped tails, and conspicuous white rumps, visible as the birds fly up, make it easy to identify them. The male also has a red patch on the nape of the neck. Many years ago, before we repaired the northeast end of the house, flickers used to come and tap at the trim boards to proclaim their territory during courtship. The tapping held no romance for me, only reminding me to get on with the work.

The worst thing I can say about our cats is that they kill things. Gusto delivers a flicker at my feet; Miso announces that she's caught something and then offers up a mouse for our appreciation before she devours it head first. Such scenes keep us constantly aware of the fragility of life. The cats also kill shrews and moles, but for some reason they don't eat them; they probably don't taste good. The strangest looking of these rodents is the star-nosed mole, *Condylura cristata*, on the end of whose nose is a ring of twenty-two fleshy pink tentacles that move as the mole searches for food. It is nearly impossible to find its tiny eyes through its rich coat of black fur.

August 31

Early this morning I went up to check the corn and found the coons had eaten and flattened most of the patch, making me swear yet again to put up that electric fence next year. I am sometimes amazed at how, despite the many failures caused by the weather, bugs, or creatures around here each year, we and most others who grow fruit, vegetables, and flowers continue to be ever hopeful and mostly undaunted. We plan and plant and perform our rituals and hope for the best; perhaps it is our sense of wonder at getting what we do from the earth that keeps us at it. Wendell Berry's poem "The Current" is eloquent on the subject of humanity and the earth:

> Having once put his hand into the ground,
> seeding there what he hopes will outlast him,
> a man has made a marriage with his place,
> and if he leaves it his flesh will ache to go back.
> His hand has given up its birdlife in the air.
> It has reached into the dark like a root
> and begun to wake, quick and mortal, in timelessness,
> a flickering sap coursing upward into his head
> so that he sees the old tribespeople bend
> in the sun, digging with sticks, the forest opening

Throughout the Summer, we have such an abundance of fresh flowers in the gardens that we always have plenty of fresh-cut arrangements in the house. Here are two late-Summer gatherings: dahlias, baby's breath, larkspur, cosmos, and variegated monkshood (top); and asters, zinnias, dahlias, scabiosa, and Salvia hormonium *(above).*

*P*ond *Island, located about a mile off the head of Cape Rosier, is our destination on the Labor Day weekend (this page and opposite). Arriving in sailboats, canoes, and rowboats in midafternoon, we gather driftwood for the campfire, collect rosehips, and get in close to the fire for a traditional picnic feast and songfest as the sun goes down and the evening chill sets in.*

to receive their hills of corn, squash and beans,
their lodges and graves, and closing again.
He is made their descendant, what they left
in the earth rising into him like a seasonal juice.
And he sees the bearers of his own blood arriving,
the forest burrowing into the earth as they come,
their hands gathering the stones up into walls,
and relaxing, the stones crawling back into the ground
to lie still under the black wheels of machines.
The current flowing to him through the earth
flows past him, and he sees one descended from him,
a young man who has reached into the ground,
his hand held in the dark as by a hand.

September 4

Lynn and I are acutely aware of the diminishing of light and heat. I am reminded of E. B. White's description of this time of year: "The tides run in and out, clams blow tiny jets of seawater up through the mud, a white line of fog hangs around the outer islands, days tumble along in cool blue succession, and I hate the word September."

Labor Day weekend had arrived; the leaves on the maple, birch, and ash trees were beginning to change color; and we sailed out to Pond Island, a few miles to the southwest, to rendezvous with friends and spend the night. When we set sail in the early afternoon, a good southwest breeze was blowing, and the bald face and rough currents at the head of the cape made for some rough sailing. Yet despite the 2-foot chop and occasional spraying of the sea, everyone took a turn at the tiller. The weather was warm and fine, the bay was deep blue, and many boats were out. We ran into our friends Kim and Deb and had an impromptu race. Finally, we sailed into a safe little inlet at the north end of Pond Island at about 4 P.M. We set the anchor and went ashore in the coracle. Carrying supplies, Tom, Kenny, and Paul arrived by canoe, rowboat, and catboat, and Peter and Deirdre set about gathering driftwood for the fire.

Tents were set up and the campfire was lit, and soon we had begun an old-fashioned picnic, with corn cooked on the open fire and mussels, clams, potato

Our blueberries are fenced in to protect them from grazing deer, porcupines, skunks, and raccoons (above).

Morning dew glistens on a cluster of plump highbush blueberries nearly ready to be picked (opposite).

salad, potato chips, and watermelon and roasted marshmallows for dessert, of course. Jugs of hard cider were emptied. As it got dark we ate, watching the fantastic orange and vermilion colors in the western sky. We sang songs that we had learned long ago at camp, like "John Jacob Jinkleheimerschmidt" and "I've Been Workin' on the Railroad." We could see some fireworks from the Blue Hill Fair, and late in the evening, we were treated to a magnificent show of "northern lights," or the aurora borealis, long, greenish-glowing columns shooting from the horizon high into the star-filled black sky. These mysterious lights are thought by scientists to be caused by "solar wind," the injection of charged particles of solar origin into the earth's magnetic field.

September 6

Today I can hear several kids chattering and laughing up in the highbush blueberries and the distinct sounds of the berries dropping into the coffee cans they wear around their necks so they can pick with two hands. After an hour or so they will proudly display their quarts and quarts of berries. Then they're off on the raft to explore the pond. We used to freeze a lot of these berries, but we have lately decided that freezing causes them to get mushy, so this year we plan to turn some into blueberry sauce before freezing. Making the sauce is simple: We just heat the berries in a saucepan until they burst, being careful to stir frequently as we watch the color change from indigo to a deep, deep blue to black and finally to purple. Then we let them cool and pop them into the freezer. Warmed blueberry sauce over vanilla ice cream is "some good," as Mainers would say.

Our highbush blueberry, known variously (and sometimes incorrectly) as whortleberry, hurtleberry, blaeberry, sparkleberry, bilberry, and huckleberry, is indigenous to North America. The plant belongs to the genus *Vaccinium*, which means "of cows" in Latin, though frankly I'm uncertain how blueberries relate to cows. These berries were held in high esteem among the North American Indians, who added them liberally to puddings, cakes, and pemmican—the Indian staple of shredded, pressed dried meat, fat, dried fruit, and berries. The berries were harvested in great quantity and some were dried in the sun and then stored indefinitely. According to one account, a favored Indian feast meal was wild duck stewed with fresh blueberries. Early American settlers valued the wood of the plants for its strength and flexibility, using it to make tool handles.

*O*ur highbush blueberries, originally planted by
Helen and Scott Nearing in the 1960s, are located
southeast of the house on a gentle slope covering a
quarter of an acre, fenced in by 8-foot chicken
wire. Children from our area come to pick the blueberries and raspberries, many of which will be sold
to Pilgrim's Inn on Deer Isle.

BLUEBERRY MUFFINS

◆

S ince Lynn is allergic to dairy products and wheat, she's come up with a simple recipe using rice and soy flour. In the Summer, we like to sit outside by the pond with our cats, breakfast, and the local paper. What a treat to have fresh blueberry muffins right from the oven.

◆

We set freshly baked blueberry muffins on a table out-side the kitchen to cool a few minutes before eating them.

1½ cups rice flour

¾ cup soy flour

2½ teaspoons baking powder

4 eggs

1½ cups soy milk

½ cup honey

1 teaspoon grated lemon rind

*¼ cup safflower oil or
favorite oil*

2 cups blueberries

◆

1.   Preheat the oven to 400°F. Grease 24 muffin tins.

2.   In a large mixing bowl, stir or sift together the rice flour, soy flour, and baking powder. In another mixing bowl, lightly beat the eggs, then whisk in the milk, honey, and lemon rind. Slowly whisk the oil and other liquids into the dry ingredients just until combined. Do not overmix. Fold in the blueberries.

3.   Spoon the batter into prepared muffin tins, filling each three-quarters full. Bake the muffins about 20 minutes, until they are a rich golden brown and a toothpick inserted in the center of a muffin comes out clean.

4.   Let the muffins cool in the pans on a rack for about 2 minutes; then turn them out onto the rack to cool.

Yield: 21 to 24 muffins

BLUEBERRY CHUTNEY

A great addition to roasted turkey or chicken or most any rice dish, this chutney brings back memories of our hot August afternoons up in the blueberry patch.

1 quart blueberries

¼ cup brown sugar

¼ cup cider vinegar

¼ cup raisins

1 teaspoon dry mustard

1½ teaspoons grated lemon rind

½ teaspoon cumin

½ teaspoon ground ginger

¼ teaspoon salt

Combine all ingredients in a heavy saucepan and bring to a simmer. Cook partially covered over low heat for 15 minutes, stirring occasionally. Cool and store in the refrigerator for up to 1 month, or put the chutney in canning jars as you would preserves.

Yield: 2½ cups

September 10

Cape Rosier is fortunate to have a state park of 1,200 acres, including 2.3 miles of shore frontage that provides the town of Brooksville with its only usable public access to the ocean. The Holbrook Island Sanctuary is not an island itself, but rather is named for the island home of the eccentric philanthropist Anita Harris, who donated the land to the state of Maine in 1971 to ensure that it would remain forever wild and to protect the wildlife there. Stories still abound about Anita Harris, who never married and died in 1985 at the age of ninety-two. A lover of animals, travel, adventure, and the outdoors, Anita Harris assembled a menagerie that included horses, cows, sheep, pigs, cats, and dogs. Miss Harris was herself a devout vegetarian: "I don't want to make a graveyard out of my stomach," she admonished her cook.

On a warm, overcast day last week I went over to Fresh Pond in the sanctuary with a couple of bird-watchers. The bird migration is mainly over, but osprey still reside in huge nests near the tops of dead trees. We were able to locate three nests, many young birds, and two pairs of adults. These huge birds, sometimes called fish hawks, have a wingspread of 4½ to 6 feet and are well adapted to catching the fish that comprise their whole diet. The osprey hovers over the water until a fish nears the surface and then plunges feet first into the water to grasp the fish with its talons. The soles of the osprey's feet are equipped with sharp, spiny projections to ensure a firm grip on the slippery prey.

We kept a respectful distance, using our binoculars to get a closer look. Nevertheless, the adult birds gave short, sharp cheeping calls to notify their young to beware. At this time of year they are encouraging their young to fly and to catch their own food, for soon they, too, will begin the migration south and all will need to fend for themselves. These birds nearly became extinct because of the use of DDT, but since its use was banned they have made a great recovery.

Continuing our walk, we spotted a pair of double crested cormorants whose hollow bones enable them to get airborne despite their large size. Later, we caught a glimpse of a red-breasted nuthatch halfway up a huge old hemlock tree.

September 15

After a few games of croquet with friends, in the late afternoon we all went down the road about a mile to Bakeman's beach to gather some mussels for dinner.

Euell Gibbons described the mussels found here as "the neglected blue mussel, one of the most delicious, most abundant, and most easily procured of all seafoods." In the Spring and Fall we have extremely low tides and high tides up to twelve feet. On this very late Summer day the tide was so low we could walk farther out to where the very large mussels grow. The big ones are three to four inches long, deep indigo blue outside, with beautiful nacreous shades of silver and pale blue to white inside. The mussels attach themselves to the rocks with strong, silklike threads called the "byssus" or "beard." As we harvest them, we grab these threads and pull toward the big end of the shell, thereby debearding them on the spot.

In no time at all we had a basketful; both we and the cats would eat well tonight. We arrived back home and gave the mussels a good scrubbing. The cats were already crowding around us.

I had recently tasted anew *moules marinières* prepared in the traditional French way, and now I was eager to try them again. Using the largest, deepest skillet we had, we sauteed onions in plenty of olive oil until they were translucent. We added two cups of white wine and filled the pan three deep with mussels, adding some bay leaves and several sprigs of fresh thyme and fresh parsley. When the mussels opened, we served them with their broth in individual bowls. We used the empty sides of the mussel shells as spoons as we ate the tender morsels, and we sopped up the delicious broth with French bread. White wine and a salad of tomatoes, feta, and olives topped it all off.

Penobscot Bay water temperatures at Summer's end are as high as they get at around 60 degrees. This body of relatively warm water has a moderating effect on our climate for the next month and a half or so, pushing back our first killing frost date sometime into the first or second week of October. These days we try to get down to the water at least once a day to see the different faces of the constantly changing tides. The tidal cycle is semidiurnal, meaning that there are two more or less equal highs and lows daily. Each day now, the high and low tides will be about an hour later than those of the preceding day—something we must keep in mind especially when we're sailing.

Native to the Maine coast, with its frigid ocean temperatures, is the American lobster, *Homarus Americanus*, the big-clawed crustacean. About half of all lobsters caught in New England are from Maine, and for the last twenty years

Gathering mussels with friends Neenah and Noah on Bakeman's beach at low tide only increases our anticipation of a fine meal of moules marinières. *The cats will also be happy because we've picked enough for all of us.*

Because of commercial overharvesting, clamming is a dying way of life on the Maine coast. But Dick Klain (top) and John Howard (above) dig clams for pleasure on Cape Rosier and get a good harvest after a few hours of backbreaking work with the clam rake.

In the still of a hot Summer's day, our rowing boat sits in the middle of our pond (opposite).

JOHN AND JANE HOWARD'S CLAM CHOWDER

If you are using hen clams, clean them first and put them through a food grinder. When digging hen clams, John Howard says you have to be fast because they have feet and hang on "like grim death to a jackass."

2 to 3 dozen hard-shell clams, scrubbed

¼ pound salt pork, diced small

2 cups chopped onions

3 cups diced potatoes

¾ pound scallops, cut in half if large

½ pound haddock, cut in 2-inch chunks

1 12-ounce can evaporated milk

1 cup heavy or whipping cream

1. In a large pot, cover the clams with cold water and bring them to a boil over high heat. Cook, covered, until the clams open, about 8 minutes. Remove the clams from their shells, chop them, and set aside. Strain the broth through a double layer of cheesecloth and set aside 3 cups.

2. In a large, heavy soup pot, cook the salt pork over low heat until the fat is rendered and bits of pork are browned. Add the onions and cook over medium heat for 5 minutes until softened. Add the potatoes and the reserved 3 cups of broth. Simmer, partially covered, for 10 minutes, or until potatoes are almost tender.

3. Add the scallops, haddock, and reserved chopped clams, along with the evaporated milk and cream. Simmer uncovered for 10 minutes.

4. Serve immediately or cool and refrigerate for a day or two to develop flavors. Gently preheat the chowder before serving.

Yield: 9 to 10 cups

When most people think "lobster," they also think "Maine," and probably half the lobsters caught in New England are caught off the Maine coast. At Hiram Blake Camp on Cape Rosier, Paul Venno and his crew—son Nathan, friend Susanna, and dog Sarah— tie up after spending a long day hauling traps.

the lobster catch in this state has remained constant at around 20 million pounds. Lobsters are caught in baited traps connected to buoys. The classic American lobster trap or pot, basically unchanged for over a hundred years, is made of hardwood slats nailed to a rectangular or half-round frame. Netting funnels lead the lobster inside to the bait, then to an inner chamber called the "parlor." In order to protect the lobster population, there are restrictions on the minimum and maximum size that may be harvested. The measurement is made with a gauge placed between the eye socket and the end of the large body shell, called the "carapace." In 1989 the minimum size was 3¼ inches and the maximum was 5 inches. Any lobsters not in that range must be thrown back into the sea. The prices paid to a fisherman in Maine for his lobsters have risen from just a few cents per pound in 1880 to $2 to $6 a pound today.

We drove over to the other side of the cape to get some lobsters for supper from Paul Venno at Hiram Blake Camp. He said he had some "culls," lobsters with only one claw, at a good price, and some "soft shells," also a bit less expensive because there's less meat in the new shell, so we brought home some of each. Tonight's dinner of lobster, corn on the cob, and a fresh tomato and arugula salad became a small celebration of late Summer—and perhaps Indian Summer, if we are fortunate. The lobsters were so good that, as Dick Klain likes to say, "They'd bring tears to a spruce plank."

September 21

The temperature at night is going down into the 40s. We are three weeks into September and the sun is setting at 6:30 P.M. We are still harvesting many flowers for cutting and for the wreaths. This year we are collecting zinnias and anthemis, which we haven't tried drying before. In our quest for variety in texture, form, and color in the wreaths, we are always looking and experimenting. The colors of the cut flowers seem to gain in intensity as the days shorten. Or do we simply notice their color more now that their days are numbered?

The Fall spinach I had dampened, chilled, and stored in the refrigerator in early August for a week prior to planting (to break dormancy) has come up. It needs thinning, and some of the thinnings will be transplanted into the greenhouse. But before we do that, we add at least five wheelbarrow loads of compost to enrich the soil there. Then the spinach can go in, along with swiss chard, bok choy, escarole, endive, and leeks. Other Fall crops are already growing well in the garden: daikon radish, Japanese mustard, celery, cauliflower, cabbage, Brussels sprouts, and broccoli. And so were the root crops: beets, carrots, potatoes, turnips, parsnips, and Jerusalem artichokes. We are ensured plenty of food to carry us into next Summer.

Late Summer fades into Fall, and on the Autumn equinox, we have 3½ hours less daylight than we had on June 21. Now, with the cooler nights and shorter days, we need to begin harvesting the Fall root crops, planting more of the ground with winter rye, building the compost pile, and cleaning up the gardens. As always, Maine Summer has been all too brief, and we have spent it in a frenzy of work and play.

Paul separates the hard, meatier lobsters from the shedders, which are cheaper and sweeter but have less meat and more water (top). Lobstering requires long hours, five or six days a week; the law mandates that Sundays be taken off. Paul has been doing this rugged work for seventeen years.

Butch Smith steams lobsters over seaweed (above) for a wedding feast at the Lookout Inn on Flye Point in Brooklin.

A cormorant airs out its wings on a mooring pole at the Bucks Harbor Yacht Club in South Brooksville (above), oblivious that Summer is officially over.

Five brave Canada geese (opposite) amaze us by landing on our pond, for the first time ever, during their migration south. Their white "chin straps," black heads, and V-shaped rump bands make them easily identifiable.

Autumn is the most beautiful of all seasons in New England. Between the green lushness of Summer and the black and white of Winter, Autumn bursts like a flare. The arrival of the Autumnal equinox means that we have days and nights of equal length. The days dawn crystal clear, and the goldenrod, New England asters, and asparagus ferns sparkle in the morning dew. The cats, frisking about more than ever, seem to appreciate the weather and the vivid colors as much as we do.

The Summer folk, or "rusticators" as Mainers call them, leave well before the foliage starts turning, and with them the insects—a blessed relief. Only the people who live here year around know how many poignant Summerlike days remain after the docks are taken down. Quiet settles on the beaches and nature seems to shift gears.

The ever-abundant garden continues to yield. We harvest storage crops and fill the root cellar with daikon radishes, potatoes, apples, cabbage, pumpkins, beets, and rutabagas. We make our sauerkraut and cider, clean up the gardens, weed and transplant perennials, plant the cover crop, and build compost piles. We may get a light frost by the end of September, particularly around the full moon, but due to the warming effects of the bay, our first killing frost generally comes in early to mid-October.

During a few blessed Indian Summer days, we enjoy the season without urgent tugs at our conscience. No longer is everything ripening all around us, as it was in Summer, when no amount of daylight, even long twilight evenings, is long enough to do everything that must be done. Unlike tomatoes, apples can wait. On brilliant Summerlike days, we take time for some exciting sailing in the bay or for long, leisurely walks. We stop abruptly at the sight of some ancient red maple, a lantern leading our way into a steadily darkening season. Fall provides such a rich palette of yellows and reds in Maine, not just the flaming maple but scarlet dogwood, blood-red oak, and the mulberry hue of white ash. We have found that the drier the Summer, the duller the colors of Autumn; but even in dry years, they are a wonder to behold against the gentian blue of an October sky.

Once again our yard becomes a feeding station for spectacular Arctic birds. The Canada geese fly noisily over our house as they did last March, but this time a gaggle of them decides to land in our pond for a brief respite. The osprey, robins, and flickers are likewise departing. Gradually, the natural sounds

Two raccoons search the shore for some unsuspecting crabs, which make up their diet along with fish, birds' eggs, vegetables, and fruits.

subside around us. The peepers hibernate; the crickets burrow deep into the soil. By mid-October the nights are so still, the sound of a barking dog in the distance is almost welcome.

In November, with all our crops harvested and carefully stored, we bank up the house to protect us from the chill winds that have once again begun to blow. Out come the long johns, as we draw closer to the wood stoves. Officially, Winter is a month away, but not by the feel of things here on Penobscot Bay. Thanksgiving time evokes great feelings of contentment. Once again we have provided abundantly, and with our own hands, for the long, cold months ahead.

September 22

The poignant smell of Autumn in the air—damp earth, wood smoke, fallen apples—signals the onset of Fall and another Summer too quickly passed. Now, night falls without twilight, like drawing down a shade, and the air that is deliciously crisp when the sun shines turns foreboding at night, too chill for the more tender plants. We hear that snow is forecast for the northern mountains of Maine tonight.

Today, the weather radio warned us of impending gale-force winds on Penobscot Bay. At 5:30 P.M., with scarcely an hour of daylight left, I hurried five hundred feet down to the water from the house, remembering that I had yet to bail out the 1½ inches of rainwater Hurricane Hugo had dumped in the sailboat last week. Since Hugo caused enough turbulence to tear rockweeds loose from the rocks, yielding almost a truckful of seaweed for the garden, I anticipate another sea-tossed harvest of mulch in the morning.

We had prepared for the hurricane by moving the boat to a better anchorage, though she took on the inevitable deluge of rainwater, and we had battened down anything around the house that could blow away. The night Hugo slammed past us, violent winds tore at the house, rattling windows. All I could do was pray to the sea gods for mercy. It was granted.

A nearby pair of loons seemed less timid than usual as I went out in the coracle to bail out the sailboat. With an hour of daylight left, the sea was flat calm like a giant peaceful lake, the sky varying shades of gray. In the bay, Islesboro was visible, but the Camden Hills behind to the west were lost in the billowing, heavy gray clouds. Not far away, I could see the sleek black heads of at

The cosmos, one of our most important cut flowers (above), seems to achieve a more brilliant color in the Fall and lasts until first frost in late September or early October.

During the early Fall, when the garden is starting to be less demanding, Lynn finds time to pull weeds from the perennials like these Artemesia ludovica *(left).*

BEEKEEPING

Our friend Rob Groves is keeping bees for the first time this year. He got interested in it not only because his family like to use honey instead of sugar, but also because he thought bees would ensure good pollination of his large gardens and small orchard. Through a local bee club, Rob met a beekeeper on Deer Isle, who gave him all the equipment he needed to get started—including a hive, a smoker, a special hive tool, a veil, and gloves—and recommended he buy *The ABC & XYZ of Bee Culture*, published by the A. I. Root Company.

To populate his hive, Rob ordered a shipment of bees, called a "bee package," from an outlet in Hayneville, Alabama. The package consisted of one queen and about 15,000 bees, all guaranteed disease-free, of which approximately 90 percent were infertile females and the remaining 10 percent were drones, or males. The queen can lay up to 2,000 eggs a day when the nectar is flowing, and only when the nectar falls off in the Fall does she stop. The drones only function is to breed with the queen. They have no stinger, and in

the late Fall, they are forced out of the hive and soon die.

This first year, Rob told us, he won't be getting any honey. All the honey in the hive must be left alone so that the bees have plenty to get them through their first winter.

Rob's hive is made up of the three boxes, or "supers" as they are called by apiarists. Because bees are very particular about the space they inhabit— hence the term "bee space"— the size of supers is standardized, so that they are interchangeable. All supers are 20 inches long by 16 inches wide. They come in three depths: full, 9⅝ inches; medium, 6⅝ inches; and shallow depth, 5¾ inches. Rob uses full depth on the bottom and medium for the two upper supers. The upper two supers are easier to manipulate; a full depth super when full of honey can weigh as much as 90 pounds.

Inside each super are ten frames, and it is on these frames that the bees build their honeycomb and deposit their nectar. There must be a ⅜-inch space between frames and between supers. Anything smaller, and the bees won't fit in; anything larger, and the bees will fill it with comb, and the beekeeper will have to pry apart the supers.

The super on the bottom has the most honey. This is the hive which is easiest for the bees to fill first, since it is where they enter. Since heat

rises, the top super will be the warmest of the three in Winter, and this is where the bees will best be able to survive. So, in Fall the bottom super which contains the most honey is moved to the top. During the Winter the bees will huddle together, in what is termed a "broodless winter cluster," in the upper super and try to maintain a temperature of 85 to 98 degrees. They will do this by quickly moving or shaking their wings; the more the temperature drops outside the faster they will need to beat their wings.

In mid-October the flow of nectar coming in from the workers has slowed down, and because of this the queen has stopped laying brood. Not many flowers are still in bloom, and she will not begin laying again until late February or early March. Before moving the bottom super Rob must remove the queen excluders to allow the queen access to the top. An excluder is a flat metal grid, its spaces large enough for the workers but too small for the queen to pass through. Several excluders are placed between the brood chambers and the honey supers to prevent the queen from laying brood in the honey super. The apiarist wants to keep the honey as pure as

possible and does not want brood or baby larvae in the honey frames.

To facilitate his work, Rob always chooses a sunny day when many of the bees are away foraging for nectar. He says that bees, like people, have moods, and on sunny days when they are able to work they are in a good mood and less likely to attack him. He follows a standard procedure: In a small metal container with an inverted funnel for a top and a bellows attached, he lights a smoky fire using dried grass and rotted wood.

Wearing only a head net,

he blows smoke into the hive. The bees think their hive is on fire and quickly gorge themselves on honey to provide the energy needed to establish a new hive. But the effect is to calm them and make them less able to sting.

Rob removes the top or telescoping cover and examines the top frames. There is not much honey in the top super, but many lower frames are oozing with golden honey. Hundreds of bees are slowly moving about, some crawling on Rob's hands. He calmly goes about his task, all the while explaining to us what he is doing,

with not the slightest worry about being stung. He does get stung every now and again, but he feels worse for the bee, since honeybees die if they sting someone. The stinger of the worker bees consists of two lancets with sharp fishook-type barbs pointing downward like a harpoon. When a bee inserts its stinger into an animal or person and tries to pull the stinger out, it invariably pulls out part of its abdominal parts with it and dies.

Various health-giving claims are made for honey and, of course, royal jelly. Bee venom has been used in the treatment of arthritis. The venom contains mellatin, which creates the pain in the sting. It also increases plasma cortisol; it's this last effect that gives relief from arthritis pain. The venom can actually be extracted by the beekeeper. An electric ramp is installed in front of the hives, and as the bees walk into the hive, they are lightly shocked, which causes them to sting a silicone cloth under the grid. The collected venom is dried, packaged, and sent to drug laboratories. Stings from 10,000 bees are needed to collect one gram of the the venom.

As Rob finishes up his work, I once again think that next Spring I'll get a hive.

In mid-September, we transplant spinach, lettuce, kale, and bok choy from the garden into the protection of the greenhouse. They usually provide us with fresh greens into January. Spinach and kale will winter over and begin growing again in early March.

GREEN TOMATO GINGER CHUTNEY

For many years, we just let the late green tomatoes sit out in the garden and freeze. But now we harvest them before the frost and either fry them breaded in cornmeal or turn them into this spicy chutney. This is very spicy with fresh ginger! It would still be spicy with even half this amount, so do adjust the ginger according to taste.

5 cups chopped firm green tomatoes (about 2 pounds)

2 cups seeded, chopped red bell peppers

1½ cups raisins

½ cup grated fresh ginger root (see above)

1 lemon, unskinned, seeded, and chopped

1 clove garlic, finely chopped

1½ teaspoons salt

¼ teaspoon cayenne pepper

2 cups packed light-brown sugar

2 cups cider vinegar

1. In a 3- or 4-quart nonreactive (nonaluminum) pan, stir together all the ingredients. Bring to a boil, stirring to dissolve the sugar. Reduce the heat and simmer, uncovered, until the ingredients are softened, about 30 minutes.

2. Remove the mixture from the heat, let it cool, then pour it into jars and refrigerate. The chutney will keep several weeks in the refrigerator and can also be frozen. The hot chutney can also be canned according to standard methods.

Yield: 2 quarts

least three harbor seals looking my way. With a light splash they humped their backs up and dove under, only to appear a few moments later about fifty yards farther from me, oblivious to the gale warnings. The Penobscot Indians hunted the seals, using sealskins for clothing and the blubber for cooking purposes. The harbor seal we know, *Phoca vitulina*, grows to about five feet long and may weigh up to 250 pounds. Any day now, the young pups will be big and strong enough to begin their slow swim southward to the warmer waters of Massachusetts and Rhode Island, and they will return again next April or May.

One Summer several years ago, Lynn and I spotted a baby seal when we took our rowboat out to Pond Island. Just as we landed, we noticed the baby seal, curled up asleep on the shore not ten feet away. We tried to be as quiet as possible pulling the boat up on shore, but we must have awakened it, for when we went to have another look, the pup was gone.

September 25

This can be a good time of year for bird-watching, and Lynn and I followed the paths on our property over to the Holbrook Wildlife Sanctuary on Cape Rosier. We walked along a well-maintained trail of soft, damp earth, the air smelling fresh of balsam fir, for perhaps a quarter of a mile before we came to Fresh Pond, where I had seen quite a few ducks and several osprey about a month ago. Osprey nests stood out against the clear blue sky near the tops of dead trees in the midst of the pond, but the birds had left for warmer climates. Terns were nesting near the salt marshes, but we were oblivious and strolled too close to their breeding grounds. They flew over our heads, crying out their high-pitched alarm until we altered our course.

Soon, it was quiet again. Suddenly, we heard the familiar honking of the Canada geese coming from the north on our left. They were right on course, heading south six months and a day after we had seen several formations winging north. A long way off, cormorants were flying about on the lookout for fish. We waited and watched, standing under a red maple tree in the process of dropping her leaves one by one into the pond. Down they gently fluttered, a colorful, whimsical surrender to the encroaching cold. Nearby some winterberry grew only a few inches above the ground. With its shiny, dark green, oval leaves,

We sell cut flowers, like the cosmos gathered here, to inns until our first frost comes in the Fall.

*During the fine days of an Indian Summer, we appreci-
ate the last of the warm weather; vivid colors of the trees
and berries, such as these rose hips (opposite); and the
tranquility of our farm (above).*

winterberry is easy to locate under evergreen trees. The white-to-reddish berries are a sweet treat that remind me of wintergreen mints.

Walking around the pond, we saw evidence that its shores were expanding. The beavers must have been working on their dams in a determined manner; the area had many freshly cut birch trees. The beavers use the trees for their nests and dams, and they eat the bark. There were fallen trees everywhere. Though we probably wouldn't get to see a beaver in the middle of the day—they are busy at dawn and dusk and through the night—the gnawed pencil points at the ends of the logs told a story of much activity. We spotted a family of red squirrels scurrying about, and we noted with no small concern the thickness of their Fall coats. The length and density of this deep auburn fur foretells a cold Winter ahead. That they are busily gathering their store for the long months ahead is another sure sign of the approach of Winter.

In the Fall, we are already thinking about future plantings, collecting and saving flower seeds for next year. Here I am picking seed from the petunias (top) and gathering Althea zebrina *seeds (above).*

There were some cattails a few feet out in the water. Euell Gibbons called these plants "the supermarket of the swamps," because no wild or domesticated plant produces a greater number of different kinds of food and material than *Typha latifolia*, the common cattail. The bloom spikes on the plants in front of us were in the process of going to seed, producing masses of what looked like feathers that aid in scattering the seeds.

The early colonists were said to have used this feathery material for insulation; knowing this I once gathered a vast amount of the fluff and stuffed a pillow with it, which remained in good shape for years. In May, I sometimes go down to a nearby swamp to gather the green bloom stalks of the cattail plants. Like ears of corn, these are enclosed in papery sheaths which must be removed before cooking. We boil the spikes for about ten minutes, then butter and eat them like ears of corn (though they taste more like cooked lettuce). A bit later in the season, it is possible to gather pollen from the bloom spikes to add to pancakes and muffins. The cattail's leaves can be cut in the Fall and dried to make rush bottom chairs. I haven't done this, but I have used the leaves to weave around water bottles, to protect them on outings, or around the glass bottles that serve as hard cider jugs.

September 30

Last night we had our first frost. Luckily, it was a light one. After hearing the warning on our weather radio, we were able to hurriedly harvest the most tender vegetables still in the garden: all the red tomatoes, a lot of the green ones, and all the peppers and eggplants.

One bright, sunny day a week ago, we gathered the winter potatoes that would take us through the coming months. Lynn and I worked our way down the rows standing opposite each other. I used a heavy-tined spading fork to unearth the potatoes, and Lynn threw them in piles where they skin over and dry for several hours in the sun before we take them down into the root cellar. This year, the early Red Norland potatoes produced very well because we got them in before the heavy rains of May and they were able to survive the long dry spell we had from early June to late July. But the winter potatoes went in late and got off to a very slow start. We only harvested three bushels instead of six or seven, reminding us once again of how much we are at the mercy of the weather.

As soon as the various gardens are stripped bare of their summer yield, we plant winter rye, broadcasting the seed and then raking it into the soil. This cover crop prevents soil erosion over the Winter and begins growing again in the Spring, providing a great deal of valuable organic matter for the soil when it's tilled back in before next year's planting.

October 4

The days seem to shorten dramatically now. Shadows lengthen as the sun's rays weaken; "beautiful light," we're always saying to one another. The colors are more vivid every day.

As I pass our maple in the fullest of its fall display, I think of Thoreau's "I would fain pluck the whole tree and carry it home for a nosegay." He observed that in Winter, trees are gray and brown, sometimes outlined with a faint touch of maroon; in Summer, an indistinguishable blend of lush foliage; but in Fall, "when they are ripe, so to speak . . . their different characters appear."

Once again, it's time to keep up with the harvesting, though not at the same hectic pace needed on a warm Summer's day when all the nearby gardens are bountiful. In the walled garden, a Jonathan apple tree the Nearings planted bears copious amounts of deep red apples that keep well. To harvest these, I put the apple ladder high into the tree and hang a canvas bag from one of the upper rungs. The bag allows me to use both hands to pick, filling four bushel baskets in a short time. Our cats always love to climb trees, but during apple picking they really seem eager to show us how much like monkeys they are. Pistachio, our fluffiest and softest, has a great time jumping from limb to limb, onto my shoulder and off again.

Into the cellar went the apples, and after a break to enjoy some freshly made borscht and rye bread, we resumed our chores, beginning to harvest the red and green storage cabbage. The cabbages were pulled from the earth, and then the root ends were tapped against the cart to knock off the dirt. The outside leaves were removed to go in the compost pile; the stems were left on. The red cabbage produced huge, tight heads, perhaps six to eight pounds apiece. I think they grew so well this year because we started them earlier than usual, in late May instead of early June. The red cabbages will be used for salad, coleslaw, and *Rotkohl*, a German dish made by sauteing some onions, chopped red cabbage,

After the first frost, we carefully lift dahlia tubers out of the ground and store them in the root cellar, ready to be divided and planted again next Spring.

The weathered gray clapboards, the golden oak, and the scarlet of the blueberry fields—these are the colors, this is the image, of Fall along Penobscot Bay.

October is the time for red cabbage. Before it is stored in the root cellar, we chop off the outer leaves and prepare some of the harvest for sauerkraut (above and opposite bottom). The ancient Chinese were said to have served sauerkraut to the workers building the Great Wall of China in 200 B.C. to keep them healthy.

apples, and a bit of honey and vinegar in olive oil. When I lived in Greece, every night in the *tavernas* they served cabbage salad, which to my taste is the very best: simply chopped fresh cabbage, with minced garlic, olive oil, and lemon.

The green cabbage will be turned into sauerkraut. We make the kraut in large ceramic crocks, first slicing the cabbage and adding, for each 5 pounds of cabbage, 3 tablespoons of pickling salt, 1 tablespoon of caraway, 1 teaspoon of juniper berries gathered from bushes out past the flagpole, and some garlic. When the crock is nearly full we cover the cabbage with a plate, put a towel over it, and place a heavy rock on top of the towel. The weight acts as a press, and this, together with the action of the salt (which draws water out of the cabbage), ensures that it is totally covered with water in a few days after sitting in the kitchen at room temperature. It is then ready to be stored in the cool root cellar. Periodically, one of us removes the very top layer, which has a bit of mold on it, and after a couple of weeks, it is ready to eat.

October 7

Yesterday the clouds lifted, and so my friend Peter and I decided to go for the year's last sail—or one of the last at any rate. There was plenty of work to do, but we agreed, "If we're gonna live out here, we've got to get our priorities straight." By the time we had gotten out our foul-weather gear, and gotten some cider, bread, and cheese together and reached the coracle, the clouds had billowed up and darkened and the wind had come up fast. Despite the whitecaps, we had our nerve up, so we paddled out to the boat. The waves were two to three feet, and it was tricky getting from the coracle into the sailboat, but we made it.

Should we go or not? Well, we could always stay in close and see how she took the wind and waves. The spray was in our faces, and as we cast off, a puff of wind grabbed us and we were off and running. Occasionally, a wave crashed over the side and I wished I'd worn foul-weather pants, but it was too late by then. "Just concentrate on the sailing," I told myself. The sun broke through every now and then, revealing the Camden hills wearing their fall colors. It felt like pure adventure, just the two of us in this little 18-foot boat dipping and rising out in the vast bay. We weren't out of control, but we couldn't have handled any stronger wind or higher seas.

There are still plenty of vegetables to harvest in Fall, such as zucchini, which line the garden wall (above).

BUILDING A CORACLE

*I*n 1978 I ran into a friend, Hugh Curran, at the laundromat in Ellsworth. He saw one of my laundry baskets, and he remarked that it reminded him of a miniature version of the boats, or "coracles" his uncle had once built in Ireland that were used for salmon fishing on the rivers. The possibility of making such a boat, based on a basket form covered with hide or cloth, really appealed to me. Hugh wasn't sure if anyone was still building coracles, but he wrote to his uncle to inquire.

Around the same time, the *National Geographic* ran an article about the Irish curragh, a cousin of the smaller coracle, entitled "The Voyage of the Brendan: Did Irish Monks Discover America?" by Tim Severin. My curiosity engaged, I began a search and was fortunate enough to locate the only extensive book on the history and design of coracles, *British Coracles and the Curraghs of Ireland*, written in 1936 by the noted small-craft historian James Hornell. Born of necessity, coracles have been made by people of many cultures for thousands of years. It is thought that only the dugout canoe predates the coracle as

a means of water travel.

Then, in June of 1986, I read an article in the *New Yorker* entitled "A Good Little Vessel" by Anthony Bailey. Eustace Rogers, the subject of Bailey's article, was reputed to be the last coracle-maker in England. I was inspired by the description of his craft and decided to build my own coracle. As a result, I visited Ironbridge on the River Severn to see firsthand what a coracle looked like and to talk with Eustace. I also wanted to see if I could locate any other builders in Wales, the main area where the craft were once in use. After some searching, I found another coracle-maker, Ronnie Davies, on the River Teifi in south Wales. Ronnie and Eustace spent many hours talking with

me about coracles, their construction, history, and use in fishing. It is thanks to their considerable knowledge, help, and enthusiasm that I have been able to carry on the tradition of coracle construction.

The British coracle is derived from the bitumen-coated guffa of Iraq and the skin-covered coracles of India and Tibet. Julius Caesar provided the first written reference to a skin-covered craft. Recounting his military campaign in Spain in 49 B.C., at a time when his communications had been cut by floods and destruction of bridges, Caesar said that he had ordered his men to make wickerwork boats covered with hides—boats of the kind he had seen on raids into southwest England. He refers to the presence of a keel and ribs made of light timbers, which indicates that he was referring to "curraghs," a close cousin of the coracle. Various Welsh writings in the Middle Ages mentioned coracles, usually covered by black bullock hides.

The coracle is an extremely shallow-draft boat, which floats on the water like a cork. As a result, it is particularly well suited for catching salmon in the shallow, rock-strewn rivers of Ireland and the border country between Wales and England. Two men would go out, one man in each boat, with a net between them. When a fish hit the net, one of the men would pull the net in along with the ensnared fish. The suitability of the coracle for river fishing was responsible for its long life: from ancient times into the 1930s. Unfortunately, the craft of coracle-making all but died out in the 1930s, when the cost of a salmon license was made prohibitively high after private landowners along the rivers (in England and Wales, the river rights belong to the landholders) claimed that the coracle fishermen were taking too many fish.

Only a few changes in coracle construction have occurred in the course of 2,000 years,

and these have varied regionally. One involved the use of sawed laths, as in Ironbridge, instead of split ash or willow branches in the lattice framework and also ash lath in the making of the gunwale, instead of plaited hazel or willow. The hide covering was replaced by flannel, made waterproof by tarring or pitching. This substitution probably took place around the time flannel began being made from mountain sheep, which became an important local Welsh cottage industry in the late sixteenth century. Flannel continued in use until the 1870s when a type of rough cotton calico replaced it. Although these new coverings needed to be coated, the weight of the boat was reduced to about half of its former 60 to 70 pounds. The dimensions of the coracle remained the same as when they were made of hide, when they were determined by the size of a single ox. The basic design continued to be that of a broad, ovate, latticed framework in the

form of a shallow, wide-mouthed basket.

After studying Hornell's book, I decided to build a "Boyne River type," which uses round material, such as willow shoots, instead of sawn or split wood, for the ribs. I have grown willow for basket-making since 1980, and I had allowed some shoots to grow for three or four years to nine to ten feet and over an inch in diameter, which will be strong enough for building a coracle.

On a piece of heavy construction paper I draw an extended ellipse measuring 3½ feet wide by 4½ feet long. I lay this template on the ground, and with an iron bar I make holes about every 8 inches, for the 32 ribs. Then I drive the sharpened ends of each willow rib into the holes leaning outwards at a slight angle.

At this point I select willow sticks—with a diameter of ¼ to ½ inch at their widest—that have first been dried in the shade for at least six months and then soaked in the pond for a week prior to use. If I used green or fresh material, the framework would later shrink and not create the tight construction the boat requires. To create the gunwale, I lay a weaver behind each rib and begin to rand these 32 weavers around the ribs in a "one over, one under" pattern, continuing to an even height of about six inches. At this point, there is an ellipse of vertical sticks connected by a ring of weaving close to the ground.

Now the ribs must be bent over so the coracle will take on its final shape. The ribs along the side, or the "thwartship," are bent over first, with the fore and aft ribs laid on top of them. The ends of the ribs are shoved into the ground next to the opposing rib on the opposite side. This completed, I lash all the crosspieces together with tarred marline of about ⅛-inch thickness. The sticky, tough marline is wound around each joint in a crisscross fashion, bringing the opposing ribs tightly together and giving the entire construction a great solidity.

To encourage the coracle to keep its shape, I lay a couple of boards over the framework and rest some heavy rocks on them. After about a week, I pry the coracle framework up from the ground and attach a canvas covering to the framework. With the frame on sawhorses and using a heavyweight #10 sailmaker's canvas, I first stretch the canvas over the frame and temporarily attach it with metal clamps. Then I trim off excess material and roll the edges up to the willow gunwale. After several adjustments of the clamps to get the canvas folds evenly spaced, I stitch the canvas to the gunwale using waxed linen thread, triangular shaped sailmaker's needles, and sailmaker's sewing palm. I find I often have to use a pair of pliers to pull the canvas as tight as possible.

After the canvas is sewn on, I make up a waterproofing mixture from a recipe given to me by a local canvas canoe builder. To make one gallon I combine the following: 43 ounces boiled linseed oil, 21 ounces paint thinner, 34 ounces porch and deck enamel, 2 ounces Japan drier, 6½ pounds silica obtained from a potter, and 2 ounces spar varnish. Using a paint brush, I apply a thick coating of the mixture, and then with a piece of spare canvas, I rub the sealant deeply into the canvas. I let this dry overnight and repeat the process again the next day. Then I give the coracle two coats of oil-based deck paint.

A final weaving to cap off the gunwale is now completed, and this is lashed to the weaving below it. The final step is the installation of a seat, which is supported in the middle by a single 2-foot-by-2-inch-square piece of spruce, notched to fit

into the ribs and fastened to the seat with a couple of dowels. The spruce seat, 8 inches by 1 inch by 3½ feet, is attached or slung from the gunwales.

Coracles are paddled, or more correctly sculled, not to the stern but rather toward the bow using a figure-eight stroke. Paddling to the side, as one does a canoe, sends it in circles.

We keep one coracle at the pond and one down at the cove. Some 6 feet long, the latter is the largest I have built so far and sometimes transports as many as three of us out to the sailboat. It makes a great lightweight dingy because of its exceptional buoyancy and it's able to handle rough seas.

Brilliant contrasts of color like this are the last we see before Winter sets in .

At the north end of Cape Rosier, we decide to duck behind Holbrook Island, check out Goose Falls and Tom Cod Cove, maybe pick up a mooring, and have some lunch. We'd only been out a couple of hours, but we felt the need to get into quieter waters for a while. That's a good part of why Penobscot Bay is such wonderful sailing ground; there's always some island or inlet to duck into. We grabbed a mooring near Holbrook Island. The wind had died down and the clouds began to break up again, giving us some sun and warmth while we ate and talked and appreciated the colors, the light, and the vitality of the place.

We imagined earlier explorers like Samuel de Champlain in 1604, sailing into these waters without charts, surprising the Penobscot Indians, who harvested their corn, beans, and pumpkins and hunted for seals, porpoise, and lobster along the rocky coast. After lunch, we rested up a while and then cast off. We were back out into the open waters and the sun had come out among the clouds, but the wind had picked up. We really flew back to Orr Cove. The waves were now a good three feet, and there was plenty of white water. We came into the mooring fast, the sails flapping madly as we came about. Peter was almost thrown off the bow, but he hung on and made a successful grab at the mooring line, and we breathed a sigh of relief. We got everything stowed away and wondered how we were going to get into the coracle. Peter put his lifejacket on and crossed himself, and I wondered if we should wait, but with the good graces of the sea gods, we got back to land feeling exuberant and drained at the same time. I guess that's the way it's supposed to be, under control but near the edge. With the sensation of the tossing sea still rocking me, I slept well that night.

October 10

Last night, with temperatures forecast to go down into the 20s, normal for this time of year, we decided to cover the remaining lettuce with a gauzelike floating row cover available from many garden equipment suppliers which will provide a few degrees of protection from freezing. It comes in a long roll five feet in width. In order for it to stay in place covering the lettuce, we needed to bury the edges with dirt about six inches on either side and at the ends. The material is so light that it floats over the plants and requires no hoops to hold it up.

The frost that night was lighter than expected, and our crop suffered no damage. We were still selling spinach, leeks, carrots, bok choy, and swiss chard, and we also had storage beets, carrots, daikon radish, kale, brussels sprouts, and broccoli in the garden for our own use. In our kitchen garden, which is sheltered by the house, calendula, geranium, petunias, and a few morning glories still bloomed, and there remained thyme, parsley, sage, tarragon, mint, and hyssop.

Near the garden wall where some sunflower seed heads drooped and dried in the morning sun, blue jays squawked overhead and darted in for a seed. A long line of Canada geese—at least forty of them—flew over this morning, way up there, honking. Yesterday, five of them flew low over the house, circled a few times and landed in the pond for the first time ever. Lynn ran inside for her camera. A slate-gray junco lit in the lilac tree. The ash tree was turning shades of deep yellow and purple, giving off an amber glow in the late afternoon light. The leaves had reached their peak for this year, and as if to make that seem even more final, the day was dark. Rain poured and the wind came up, blowing the sodden leaves from the trees. A day for nostalgia, made cheerful by closing in around the wood stove with a steaming mug of cider laced with rum.

October 15

Many of the trees have lost their leaves, the goldenrod has gone to seed, but some pale blue New England asters linger and the blueberry barrens are a deep and brilliant crimson. Our pond looks dark and cold, reflecting the spruce trees and the amber highlights of leaves on the wild rose and willow bushes. It is a time for working indoors, making leek soup, bottling rhubarb wine and sparkling cider, making some fruited sourdough rye bread, and beginning to saw up the firewood. It's time for us to press apples for cider over at Tom Hoey's house in South Brooksville. (Tom is on the verge of going into the business of selling hard and sparkling cider.)

The apple harvest was light this year because many of the trees from which we make cider bear heavily only every other year. And we had the added problems of a wet Spring and less than perfect germination. It takes about seven cheeses (layers of apple pulp wrapped in cloth) to make up a good pressing, and that requires at least eight grain bags, so Tom and I agreed to combine our apples in order to achieve a good blend.

We drove over to Tom's and unloaded the bags of apples from the bus to the shed. I dumped the apples into a hopper, which funneled them to the pulp mill,

MAKING HARD CIDER

Making cider is one of Fall's rituals I enjoy most. Not only is it very satisfying to press many pounds of apples until they yield gallons of the sweet, golden juice, but I look forward to turning it into scrumpy, or hard cider. This home brew has added its own special sparkle to many a happy occasion. Every year in mid-October, we drive over to Tom Hoey's cellar in South Brooksville to press our apples.

What we look for is a blend of apples which will give us a balance of sugar content, tannin, and acid. As the juice flows from the press (at this stage, it is called "must"), it is made up of 75 to 90 percent water, several sugars (glucose, levulose, and saccharose), malic and other acids, tannins, pectin, starch, albuminoids, oils ash, nitrogenous substances, and trace elements. The amount of sugar in the apples varies from year to year and from one variety to another. The must contains 5 to 10 percent sugar, most of which is converted to alcohol in the fermentation process. The malic acid in the juice helps protect the cider from the invasion of harmful bacteria and promotes the normal development of the natural yeast.

Before pressing, we leave the apples in grain bags for ten days softening, or "sweating," as it is called. This not only makes them easier to grind, it also increases their sugar content and enhances their flavor. One grain bag weighs nearly one hundred pounds, and about five and a half bags will yield about thirty gallons. Usually, Tom has gathered more apples in case I don't have enough to make up the seven cheeses, or layers, that we will press. Meanwhile, Tom's pigs, Poopsie and Sneakers, follow our progress. They are happy after the pressing is over, when they get to eat all the pulp.

Before pressing, an apple grinder powered by a 2 horsepower motor—a machine properly called a "hammer mill"—makes a mash out of the apples. Juice begins to flow almost as soon as the apples are fed into it. The mill has no blades, which could easily become dull, but rather steel flails that literally beat the apples to a pulp, or pomace. The finer the pulp, the more the juice.

Tom's press is made of oak. A reinforcing steel frame runs up the sides and over the top to stabilize the press under the great amount of pressure exerted by a 12-ton ratchet jack. This jack sits on a 1½-foot-thick oak platform, which in turn presses on the seven layers of apple pulp. Each layer consists of a heavy-duty nylon cloth that holds the pulp and a rack, which is a latticework 30 inches square reinforced by ¼-inch slats, to give it stability and spread out the weight on the press.

With only the weight of the seven layers of pulp stacked up on the press, we get about twelve gallons of cider. Once the jack is on top of the oak plate above the layers and the oak beam, the press is activated. As soon as the 12 tons begin doing their job, the deep golden juice flows in earnest. Twenty, twenty-five, thirty gallons, and the press slowed down. We ended up with a hair under thirty-five gallons from about 700 pounds of apples, about the same as other years. The wrung-out pressings were red-brown and as dry as 24,000 pounds of pressure could get them, looking like faintly dampened cardboard, but Poopsie and Sneakers were happy with their treat.

We always fill a few jugs to freeze until next year's haying in early July. Then we pour the rest, about thirty gallons, into two 15-gallon stainless steel barrels. Using a hydrometer, I add enough sugar to bring the reading up to 1.08. This will eventually yield a finished cider of about 10 percent alcohol. Since apples contain their own yeast, it is not necessary to add any to the cider for fermentation. When each barrel is full, I seal it off with a rubber stopper and airlock, which allows the carbon dioxide to escape while preventing oxygen, alien yeasts, or fruit flies from getting at the fermenting cider.

After a day or two the water in the airlock begins to bubble furiously. A couple days later the bubbling slows down and continues this way until all the sugar being acted on by the yeast has been converted to alcohol. This can take up to six months in a cool cellar such as ours; it is said that a slow fermentation provides a better end result.

When fermentation has stopped, I turn the still cider into sparkling cider. At night I mix a packet of wine yeast with 1 quart of water and 4 tablespoons of sugar. The next day I put 1 teaspoon of the yeast mix and 1 teaspoon of sugar in 1-liter bottles, then fill each bottle with hard cider and cork it. Care must be taken to use champagne bottles or heavy-

duty beer bottles that can withstand pressure; the addition of the yeast and sugar at this stage causes the cider to resume fermenting. But since the bottles are corked, there is nowhere for the CO_2 to go, so it forms the bubbles one finds in champagne or sparkling beverages.

BUILDING COMPOST

Composed of partially decomposed leaves, garden clippings, twigs, and even vegetable peelings and scraps of newspaper, compost is valuable not only to successful gardening but also to our need to recycle. (Leaves and garden waste comprise anywhere from 15 to 20 percent of our landfills.) Ripened compost adds nutrients and stable humus to the soil and improves its water-holding capacity, drainage, and aeration. Compost fosters the formation of protective organisms, antibiotics, auxins, and other biotic substances. While it can take nature 1,000 years to build an inch of topsoil, we attempt to do it in a matter of weeks.

We build our compost piles out behind the walled garden in the same area—and with the same arrangement—Scott Nearing used. He peeled the bark from 6-foot poles between 2 inches and 4 inches in diameter. To create a frame for the compost, he stacked the poles log-cabin style to a height of 3 to 4 feet. This frame contains the pile and most importantly allows air to get at its sides as the pile is built.

We try to build three piles a year so that new material can be added to the most recent pile and older compost can be allowed to decompose. Between late Summer and mid-Fall we have the most material on hand because of our harvest schedule.

To begin a compost pile, we place a layer of cornstalks on the ground to provide an aerated base. We build layers of material up to 4 to 5 inches thick, following the Indore method invented by the father of organic gardening, Sir Albert Howard. Sir Albert found layering different organic materials tended to induce decomposition and shortened the time it took to produce finished compost. Therefore, in building the pile, it is important to pay attention to the materials used in order to attain a proper carbon/nitrogen ratio. For example, old or matured plant tissue that goes into the composting process consists mainly of carbonaceous compounds such as cellulose and lignin, but it contains very little nitrogen or water. Young green plant material and seaweed contains more water, more nitrogen, and a number of organic compounds which break down more quickly than old plant tissue.

A good rule of thumb is that roughly equal amounts of rich and poorer plant materials make for good fermentation and fine compost. To our piles we add layers of kitchen waste, green matter from the garden (the roots, stems, and leaves of plants after they have been harvested), comfrey leaves or fresh-cut grass, old hay from the previous season, seaweed, a 2-inch layer of earth, and some limestone and rock phosphate.

As the organic matter in the pile breaks down or is digested and turned into usable garden humus, a great deal of heat is generated. The materials actually "cook" at temperatures higher than 150 degrees Fahrenheit. To attain these temperatures, it is best to build the pile all at once rather than adding a little bit at a time, hence the need for three piles. It is also a good idea to aereate the pile, which facilitates aerobic decomposition, by placing stakes in it. Care must be taken to keep the materials in the pile evenly distributed so the center is not higher than the sides. We build the piles to about four feet, and they settle to perhaps three feet.

When a pile is finished, we top it off with a thick layer of hay to encourage water to run off it over the winter and to prevent leaching of valuable nutrients. Some people turn their piles, but we have found this to be unnecessary. They are always broken down and ready to use by the following Spring.

where the whole apple is reduced to pomace. Tom began forming up the cloths full of pomace with a frame on top of each cheese, and we caught the flowing juice in buckets, tasting one of nature's perfect drinks as we worked. The fresh, deep amber cider was wild tasting—not the bland store-bought stuff of sweet eating apples like McIntosh or Delicious, but the rugged, hardy, tangy taste of apples, many of which are too tart to eat. William Coxe, the nineteenth-century authority, wrote that "toughness, dryness, a fibrous flesh, and astringency" were the marks of a good cider apple, and I agree. The apples we gather each year have these characteristics.

The bitterness of most of the apples we were pressing indicated high tannin levels, sure to exercise antiseptic action against the diverse bacteria that attack cider and can turn it to vinegar. Over the past seven years that Tom and I had been making cider, we had been fortunate and had not concocted anything that was undrinkable, though some years had given us better tasting cider than others. Our biggest problem seems to be to keep ourselves from overdrinking.

Each year as we work, we hold the same discussions on the merits of old varieties such as Roxbury Russet, Golden Russet, Dolgo Crabapple, Westfield Seek-No-Further, Sweet Winesap, Ashmedes Kernel, English Beauty, Coles Quince, and more. And we debate the merits of standard versus semi-dwarf or dwarf trees: The standards are much larger and take longer to mature, but their lifetime is much longer, and they are deeper rooted, giving them more protection against the Maine Winters. We talk of mouseguards and borers and of organic versus chemical orchards. Tom has planted over a hundred trees in the last few years since he decided to go into the cider business, but it will be a long time before they will be producing—seven to ten years for the standard trees.

After pressing out 35 gallons of cider, we took a tour through his ever-improving cellar. He had recently whitewashed the granite walls, and the 55-gallon oak barrels stood out sharply, waiting to be filled with this year's harvest. Tom pulled out a bottle of 1985 sparkling cider, and we repaired to his kitchen for some good drink and more talk of apples, the weather, and the harvest.

October 28

We are now in the pleasant throes of an Indian Summer, with sunny days and temperatures up in the high 60s. The National Weather Service broadcasts over

In preparation for cider pressing, we need to collect several grain bags of apples (top). To reach the highest branches of the apple trees, I use a pole to shake the apples down, though many wind up in the small stream behind the walled garden (above).

*F*all wreaths have their own special fragile grace. This assortment shows the different looks that can be achieved by varying the materials. Lynn calls one the "birchbark wreath" (top); she got inspired by a walk in the woods one morning: birch bark, pine cones, grasses, sea lavender, mosses, barberry, Nigella pods, sage, and poppy seeds. Giving off a wintry glow (above), this wreath is decorated with sea lavender, sage, artemisia, hydrangea, white statice, Nigella pods, and mosses.

NOA weather radio, and we listen at least twice a day. They told us that we were in the midst of a huge "Bermuda High," reaching seven miles up and keeping the cold air from the north at bay. I wanted to get out on the water. Brett, my neighbor, has been combing the beaches for years now, one of his favorite pastimes, and his backyard is a testament to his scavenging skills and to his eye for the practical. He has a fine collection of beams in various lengths and girths, mooring poles, styrofoam floats, lobster buoys, rusty bolts and chains, and a huge, ancient anchor, which he got from Crotch Island off Stonington.

We set out in his 11-foot flat-bottom wood boat with a small motor. It was a glorious day and about as calm as it can get. The oaks still wore their rusty orange-brown leaves; we still hadn't had a severe frost, which is unusual. Indian Bar on Cape Rosier where Brett moors his boat is at the north end of Holbrook Island Sanctuary and only about a mile by water from Castine.

Two hours before low tide, there was just enough water to get through between Ram and Holbrook Islands, heading south toward Goose Falls. This place feels pristine and mostly untouched by people, its tree-covered hilly terrain filled primarily with evergreen and some birch and oak. Along Cape Rosier one sees almost nothing but the rocky shore and trees, the few summer cottages half hidden until we come around to Harborside. Seagulls soar high overhead, probably looking for mackerel, but along the shores there is not much for the beachcomber today. We moved down towards the head of the cape and then crossed out to Western Island, where we went ashore.

Kip Leach, who lives nearby, told me that when Jarvis Green (Helen Nearing's closest neighbor) was alive, he used to trap raccoons on the cape and then row them out to this uninhabited island. They thrived on its great mouse population and the wild berries and rosehips. He then retrapped them in the Fall and sold their skins. Western Island could certainly use some predators today to thin out its overpopulated mouse colony.

When we pulled into the horseshoe cove on the north side, the water was so clear we could see lots of huge four- to five-inch hen clam shells, crabs scurrying about, sand dollars aplenty, and blue mussels clinging to the rocks. Western Island is perhaps ten acres in size, its interior covered with large spruce trees. There's a fine trail across the island, where spicy sprays of feathered spruce have laid down an ancient, deep accumulation of spruce needles to walk on. The feeling among these big, old, dark, and many-branched trees is of a quiet, sacred place; they rise like spires.

Some rosehips could still be found on the *Rosa rugosa* bushes, and I devoured these tart berries like a bird, spitting out the hairy seeds. I also nibbled some salty, succulent, gray-green goose grass and honey mushrooms, *Armillaria mellea*, which I ate raw, though Brett wouldn't. Had we been stranded on this island, we could have survived for quite a while and probably not even lost that much weight—although Brett would have had to give up his vegetarianism to survive on some mussels and clams.

On the way back we stopped at neighboring Pond Island for a quick look at the skeleton of an ancient 90-foot-long schooner lying mostly buried in the sand, its huge ribs and keel preserved by the salt water. Brett observed how it might well have been a member of one of the last great whaling fleets common in these parts during the last century. As the industry diminished, so too did the size of the craft plying the trade, going from great three-masters to the smaller schooners, such as the one beached here.

About thirty yards off our bow we saw two dolphins swimming along, their glistening black backs humping out of the water. The cormorants had left for warmer waters, but we did see many black ducks and a few seals. The sun was almost down at 5 P.M., and it was getting cold as we arrived home, just as the last light faded. It was time to get back indoors to fire up the wood stoves and think about "suppa."

October 31

Although the end of October had arrived, there was still plenty of work to do in the garden. Now, we had to remove all the dead plants to the compost pile, weed and trim back the perennials, and try to remove unwanted comfrey and nettles. Both of these are valuable plants, but they are also invasive. Once started somewhere, they tend to proliferate and are hell to get rid of. To eliminate them, special care is required to avoid breaking off any part of their roots, for even the smallest piece will grow into a new plant.

If we have a mild Fall, by November the lettuce we planted in mid-August will be full sized, and the spinach planted around the same time will still be thriving. Our hardier vegetables, able to take the frost, continue to grow. We give

The predominant flowers here (top) are apricot and pink statice, combined with touches of blue delphinium, yarrow, artemisia, German statice, and vetch, which gives it a loose, wild look. A freestyle wreath (above) is made from spruce branches covered with lichen, barberry, birchbark, Nigella pods, Celosia, and pink and purple statice.

We planted the onions from sets in early May, harvested them on a sunny August day when the tops had withered, and allowed them to cure upstairs in the barn until late October, when we braided them. Not only are the braids appealing, but they also make the onions easier to store for the Winter ahead.

the kale and brussels sprouts, which improve in the colder weather, a thick layer of hay mulch around the base to protect their roots from the freezing and thawing action as well as from the wind.

This year we harvested a bushel of daikon radishes. Huge, pure white, and phallic-looking, these radishes—some as much as eighteen inches long—are crisp and fresh, with a juicy, peppery flavor. The Japanese, whose diet includes much daikon, say that if you're going to eat a lot of rice you have to eat this, too. Because Lynn is allergic to wheat, we rely heavily on rice and also daikon. Daikon, which is translated as "large root," contains diastase, an enzyme that aids in the digestion of starches. It is said that the Japanese have at least a hundred ways of preparing daikon. We enjoy it mostly raw in salads or grated with a little fresh ginger and tamari or soy sauce.

Tonight, the usually pitch-black landscape is mysteriously flickering with the slitted eyes and sagging grins of softening jack- o'-lanterns, their gold-orange candles glowing through frosted windowpanes. Sturdier, round pumpkins—some weighing over twenty pounds—take up residence on graying porches, crowd onto windowsills, or are perched opulently atop fenceposts and walls in the towns and along the countryside.

According to Celtic tradition, this night marks the transition from Autumn to Winter. Known as Halloween, it is the evening when the souls of the departed are supposed to revisit their old homes in order to warm themselves by the fire and comfort themselves with the good cheer provided for them. It was a natural thought, perhaps, that the approach of Winter should drive poor, shivering, hungry ghosts from the now barren fields and leafless woodlands into the shelter of cottages with familiar hearths.

This year, we celebrated the hallowed eve at Edge Hill in Sedgewick, about seven miles away, where our friends Kim and Deb had made preparations at their house for a scary eve. Among the ghosts and ghouls were some strange creatures—a half-chicken/half-woman and a walking apple tree haunted by its wife in the guise of the deadly apple borer. A retired fisherman remarked that the place name, Sedgewick, means "Witch of the Marshes." He cackled menacingly at the children, who shrieked in delight. Soon, the voice of a more contemporary shaker, Jerry Lee Lewis, rattled the timbers while we danced the late hours away. We truly appeased the ancient ones this night.

Halloween is said to be the time when spirits of the dead visit their old homes, and it is incumbent on the living to appease them with warmth, comfort, and good cheer. On that hallowed eve, the only light in our house comes from jack-o'-lanterns (top). Among the ghosts and dancers at our Halloween party were some pretty unusual characters (left and above).

We save the seeds of buttercup squash and pumpkin so that we have enough to plant next year and to eat now. When they've been roasted a couple of hours on top of the wood stove, we top them with soy sauce.

PUMPKIN PIE

◆

When Halloween comes round, we usually decorate the stone wall with variously shaped pumpkins. To us, they symbolize harvest. Some we carve into jack-o'-lanterns, and then Lynn uses the meat to make into pies. Any leftovers she freezes for use in the Winter as puddings, soups, and breads.

◆

3 cups cooked and pureed pumpkin or canned pumpkin puree (see Note)

¾ cup honey

2½ teaspoons molasses

3½ teaspoons ground cinnamon

1½ teaspoons ground ginger

¼ teaspoon ground cloves

1 cup evaporated milk, soy milk, or heavy cream

4 eggs, lightly beaten

Pastry for a deep 10-inch pie pan

◆

1. Preheat the oven to 400°F. If you are using fresh or frozen pumpkin puree, drain it well.

2. In a large bowl, whisk together the pumpkin puree, honey, molasses, cinnamon, ginger, and cloves. Whisk in the milk and then the beaten eggs. (If you wish a very smooth filling, combine ingredients in a food processor.)

3. Line the pie pan with the pastry and crimp the edges to make a rim. Pour the pumpkin mixture into the prepared shell. (It will be very full.)

4. Bake the pie in the lower center of the oven for 10 minutes, then reduce the oven to 350°F and bake an additional 40 to 45 minutes, until the filling is puffed and a knife inserted off-center comes out clean.

5. Cool the pie on a rack. Serve it with ice cream, whipped cream, or yogurt.

Yield: One 10-inch pie

Note: To cook a fresh (about 4-pound) pumpkin, remove the peel, stringy portions, and seeds, cut the flesh into chunks about 3 inches, and place the chunks in a pot filled with water to cover. Bring to a boil and cook 12 to 15 minutes, until the pumpkin is very tender. Drain the pumpkin well, then puree it in a food processor, put it through a food mill, or mash it by hand. If freezing, pack into plastic quart containers or freezer bags.

PUMPKIN AND LEEK SOUP

I think pumpkins and leeks are two very important vegetables to grow for the Fall garden, when we need to be eating hearty food and fortifying ourselves for Winter. Leeks are a rugged member of the onion family and can withstand freezing temperatures, especially if they have been mulched around their base. Pumpkins are very high in Vitamin A and just plain fun to grow, carve, and set on the shelf—and of course they make delicious pies and soups.

4 tablespoons olive oil

1 large onion, chopped

5 leeks, cleaned and sliced (white and pale green parts only)

3 cups pumpkin or other winter squash such as Hubbard or butternut, cut in 1-inch cubes

3 cups frozen corn kernels

2 cups frozen lima beans

2 cups sliced green cabbage

4 tomatoes, coarsely chopped

8 cups chicken or vegetable broth or water

3 cloves garlic, pressed or minced

2 tablespoons honey

3 to 4 teaspoons tamari, to taste

¼ teaspoon freshly grated nutmeg

Freshly ground black pepper to taste

1. Heat the oil in a large soup pot. Saute the onions and leeks over medium-low heat until they are softened and lightly browned, about 15 minutes. Add the pumpkin, corn, lima beans, cabbage, and tomatoes, and cover with the broth or water. Bring the mixture to a simmer and add the garlic, honey, tamari, nutmeg, and pepper.

2. Simmer the soup, uncovered, over low heat for 30 minutes. Taste and adjust seasonings, if necessary, before serving.

Yield: 12 cups

After we harvest the pumpkins in the beginning of October, we make some into spicy pies. Others are set on the garden wall before we carve them into Halloween jack-o'-lanterns.

BASKET-MAKING

I have always been fascinated by all things woven of any kind of fiber—silk, wool, cotton, linen, willow, ash, or hemlock—for they integrate the elements of utility, texture, and color with great strength in relation to weight. I first learned to make baskets while living on a farm on the island of Skiathos in Greece. I chanced upon a basket-maker in the town of Olympia in the Peloponnese to whom I immediately wanted to apprentice myself, but I spoke almost no Greek and so continued on my way. By coincidence, six months later I was living on a farm and the farmer next door was a basket-maker. I spent many afternoons with him learning how to split bamboo, gather olive shoots, and weave baskets.

Upon returning to the United States I continued basket-making. I first used the willow and dogwood I was able to find growing wild along rivers. In 1981, a friend who was studying basket willow culture sent me some cuttings

from Belgium and France, and a friend, Brian Winn, and I planted these in my walled garden in the Spring. Some of the varieties did very well, and I still grow them. I now use willow from our garden for making baskets and coracles.

The wood for making wicker-type baskets must be cut and then dried in a shady place for six months to a year before it can be used to give it a chance to shrink. I usually cut the sticks either in late Fall or in early Spring before the sap rises, so the material is already in a drier state. Before making a basket, I soak the dried material in the pond or bathtub for four or five days and then allow it to dry out for a day.

In making a round or oval basket, I select the sticks which will be used as ribs and the ones to be used as weavers. As a rule, the weavers are always of a smaller diameter than the ribs, and the initial weavers— those to be used at the base— are the smallest diameter of all. To make the onion basket pictured here, I choose four sticks of similar size (about ³⁄₁₆ of an inch in diameter) and cut a slit in the center of each of them. I then run four sticks perpendicularly through the slitted sticks, forming a cross. To prevent the slits from enlarging and to hold the eight sticks together, I wind a willow weaver tightly around the perimeter of the square. I then spread the sticks out so the square becomes a circle. Now

I'm ready to begin the actual weaving process.

Using very small and flexible weavers, I begin an "over one, under one" design known as "wicker weave." When the bottom is completed, I cut a small slit in each rib where it must make the sharp bend to go up the side. After bending up the ribs, I secure them with a string at a point near their tops. To reinforce the junction between the bottom and side, I switch to three-strand weaving—two over and one under—to give added strength to the basket at this point. After three or four rounds of

three-strand weaving, I go back to two-strand weaving and continue up the side, always paying attention to the overall form of the basket.

When the basket reaches the desired height, I put in the handle using a fid (a wooden-handled tool with a pointed iron rod) to open up the weaving, inserting the handle ends as far down into the weaving as possible. The upper rim of the basket is completed by bending the ribs over and weaving them into a three-strand rope weave.

Many of the crops we plant will survive the early frost of Fall and even improve in sweetness, including leeks, bok choy, daikon radishes, and rutabaga (above).

Gliding so close to the water in Orr Cove in the still of dusk (opposite), it was hard not to feel part of nature.

November 15

Last night Lynn cooked down the last of the pumpkins for future pies. The pumpkin is cooked until soft, then drained and frozen. We save the seeds—some for planting, some to roast on the woodstove for snacks.

Although today is warm, we can't forget that next winter's firewood needs to be cut and split; the rhubarb wine is ready to be bottled, along with some cider we made in 1988; there are piles of seaweed and oak leaves on the beach that must be brought up and spread around the perennials; and the leeks must be transplanted to the greenhouse to protect them from the severe cold. The Bay School Craft Fair will be held in early December, and we need to make extra wreaths to sell there.

Taking advantage of this unseasonably warm day, we decided to set aside our chores and get out on the water in our kayaks. We put the kayaks into a few inches of water, attached the spray skirts to the combing around the cockpits and were ready to shove off.

The kayaks we have are called "downriver boats" by their builder, Earl Baldwin of Orrington, Maine. Several feet shorter than sea kayaks, they aren't built for long-distance voyaging on the ocean, since there is very little storage space. Nevertheless, they do very well for our forays along the coast and out to nearby islands. We are new to kayaking, but it does not take long to get the feel of it, and each time we go out we venture a little farther from our cove.

With an hour to go before sunset, we glided out of Orr Cove. There was a fairly strong breeze coming up, and we heard and saw loons not more than fifty yards ahead. Sitting inches above the water, we felt a part of the nature around us, a wave breaking over the bows, rolling up and off our boats' backs, the seawater occasionally spraying our faces. The cold gray granite ledges stood out in bold relief against the darkening orange-red sky. We were excited to be on the water this late in the year.

November 22

Old Man Winter came barreling in on a wild Nor'easter yesterday. It began raining about midnight; then the temperature dropped suddenly and the barometer hit a new record low. Snow stuck to the trees, the house, everything it

An unexpected, wild Nor'easter surprised us by dropping a foot of snow; many of the trees ended up with six heavy inches of it weighing down their branches.

touched, and the winds whipped up a frenzy, hitting 65 miles per hour at times, and suddenly we were into a major storm.

Because there was no frost in the ground to hold the tree roots—by now they had six inches of heavy snow on their branches—trees were toppled over by the gale-force winds. Many of the trees fell on the power lines, so the phones, the lights, and everything else that runs on electricity went out. Once we accepted the fact that we weren't going anywhere, it was quite cozy being by the wood stoves, looking out at the gathering storm. The weather radio told us that the winds on Mt. Washington in New Hampshire were 110 miles per hour and the temperature was −11 degrees. Visibility was down to perhaps fifty feet. The cats hugged the stoves.

Our neighbor Mark came by on cross-country skis, reporting a tree down on his phone line, which the plowman in his sanding truck had inadvertantly hit. We drank some tea and talked of storms, skiing, and all the jobs we hadn't yet done, like harvesting the late-Fall vegetables or getting enough kindling into the woodshed. When I went out into the garden, it felt as if I were in Siberia, snow swirling all around me and the wind in a howl. I decided to venture out to harvest the last of the bok choy, which was half frozen. It was the last of our lettuce, except for what we had in the greenhouse. By 4:45 P.M., it was time to light the candles and settle in for a cozy night, tuning in "All Things Considered" at 5 P.M. on our battery-powered radio. The night was just right for a New England boiled dinner—turnips, carrots, onions, and potatoes sliced up and cooked in the pressure cooker for fifteen minutes. This simple but delicious dinner made us reflect on the value of root crops, root cellars, candlelight, wood heat, and days past. We played cribbage and crawled into bed at 8:30 P.M.

If we were surprised by the first snowfall of the year, the kittens really had a hard time figuring out what to make of their first snow.

November 30

We celebrated the last day of November with a first skate on the pond, which thanks to an early blast of Arctic air suddenly had four inches of ice. As the sun was setting, I strapped on my racing skates, the cats watching and wondering what I was about to do. Lacing the skates up tight, off I went on the long blades. It felt like only yesterday, instead of ten months ago, that I was skating—glide, push, glide—the ice black, and nearly perfect.

The spruce trees were silhouetted black against the sky as I glided around and around, the sound of the blades digging into the ice as I pushed off, one foot crossing over the other in a gentle turn. The cats tried the ice but couldn't figure out why they couldn't stop without sliding or why they couldn't even get off to their usual fast start.

After nearly an hour, I could feel my feet getting sore and my ears were almost numb with the cold. I thought back to only a month ago when we were having lunch by the pond—what a transformation! It felt damn good to sit down and take off the skates and slip on comfortable boots. Sitting there in the dark, I heard the ice groan and creak, as if it were saying: Winter has come. Now is time for a rest.

I walked down to the mailbox in the dark, admiring the stars, the vast sky, and the quiet, not a single sound except my boots crunching on the frosty lane. Leafless branches were silhouetted against the last light on the horizon. Winter had indeed set in.

winter

Winter seems to be the longest season at the farm. Because of the cooling effect of the bay (above and opposite), it lasts from late November until April. Yet, it includes brilliant snowy days in which to cross-country ski and, more than likely, take advantage of some good ice for skating.

Of the four seasons, Winter is the longest, from late November until April, when the ice finally disappears from the pond. Winters are unusually harsh in Maine, thanks to the particular combination of the cooling effects of the North Atlantic and the frigid north winds which blow down from Labrador. It seems fitting that the first pair of earmuffs was patented in Maine or that the first day of Winter has been designated in honor of their inventor, Chester Greenwood. Yet, in spite of that, Winter on the Maine coast is much more variable than I could have imagined. One day it's 10 degrees below; the next the thermometer rises up into the 40s. On a recent day in January, a new record of 58 degrees was set—"downright balmy," says our neighbor Gib.

Because of the vagaries of the weather, Maine requires great flexibility from its inhabitants. We may get a foot of snow one day and spend most of the next

A foot of new snow is perfect for cross-country skiing over the logging trails and hiking paths crisscrossing the woods and fields behind our house.

plowing and clearing paths. Twenty-four hours later, pressure builds and we get wild northwest winds which blow the snow back onto the paths and driveway. A few days later, the wind switches around to the south and everything melts, only to freeze once again that night, so the truck gets stuck in the yard, the car doors won't open, and our feet go out from under us on the icy path.

These contrasts make us aware of our vulnerability as in no other season. Our sauna becomes not a luxury but a vital necessity, as it is in many countries in higher latitudes. The incredible heat followed by a dip down through the hole in the ice and a dash back into the heat warms us to the marrow of our bones.

Since the pleasures of the outdoors must be made to fit into the few daylight hours during which we can endure the cold, our community becomes an even greater source of comfort. During Winter we develop our deepest relationships with neighbors, visitors, and friends while eating and drinking around a blazing fire.

Once our wood fires are lit in late October, they don't go out until Spring. Let it snow, let the power go out, let a great storm drop a foot of snow on us. There's no better place on earth than by our roaring wood stove. We spend many hours there planning next year's garden, the colorful pages of the seed catalogs spread open on the table. For dinner we'll go down to the root cellar to gather ingredients for a feast of baked potatoes, cabbage salad, and applesauce, accompanied by rhubarb wine and candlelight.

Month after month, Winter goes relentlessly on, with a reprieve of a thaw in January or February, until late March, when the Canada geese fly over on their way north. They are the Maine coast's Spring harbingers and the cue to start our seeds indoors once again for another season of hope and plenty.

December 3

A record low of 6 degrees was set two days ago, and a winter storm watch was issued. Snow began falling on the night of December 2, and by daylight we had a foot. The scene was every man's Winter fairy tale, although skating on the pond out back was over for a while; we would have to wait for the sun to melt off the snow or for a sudden rain storm to wash it away.

With the intense cold weather and the foot of snow, I could tell that cross-country skiing would be great. It was a real treat to be able to put on our skis at

At this time of year especially, we cherish our sauna ritual (left), steaming up and taking a quick plunge into the water beneath the ice (above)—and then back to the sauna once more.

RAG-RUG WEAVING

Gail Disney has been weaving rag rugs at her studio in South Brooksville since shortly after she arrived in Maine from Pennsylvania in 1975. It was natural for her to pick a craft as a way of making money in the country because she wanted to do "something where heart, head, and hand work in harmony." At that time the center of town consisted of only the grocery store, the gas station, and a small weaving shop; but South Brooksville was, in fact, a small weaving center. The shop's proprietor, Mary Chase, had studied weaving in Sweden, where the craft is still vigorously pursued, and she imported Swedish looms, wools, and linen. At the shop, women wove the textiles which Mary designed and sold. Gail spent her last dollars to buy one of Mary's looms, a Gesta. She still uses this well-made horizontal floor loom, which relies on an intricate system of counterbalances to maintain the tension required for weaving rugs.

Weaving is the interlacing of two sets of threads, the active weft crossing the passive warp at right angles. Basically, a loom is nothing but a device to produce the necessary tension. The horizontal frame loom which Gail uses is of ancient design. It was known in Syria before A.D. 256; and it appeared in Europe around A.D. 1000. It is in Scandinavia that this type of loom has become most accepted for weaving both pile and flat rugs. Gail says that her loom is made just as one was in the Middle Ages. Sturdy, quiet, and easily taken apart, it is joined together only with wooden wedges.

We are in her post-and-beam studio built a few years ago by her husband, Tom. It is well-lit, and besides her loom there are masses of rags cut in strips and hung from posts, boxes of new cotton cloth, and colorful balls of rolled-up cotton strips. Gail decided to make cotton rag rugs of the type often produced in northern Europe. These rugs can be made of readily available material, they can be machine washed, and they can be made of brighter colors than those generally used in other types of rug weaving. Gail is able to buy cotton from the mills near Augusta, and she likes the range of colors available to her from these sources. But any type of cotton material is usable. Friends know that Gail can use old cotton sheets and clothing, and they often provide her with material.

In preparing to make a rug, Gail cuts the material into strips 1½ inches wide and 2 yards or less long. Because she uses cotton, she can make the first cut with scissors and then tear the rest. If she used synthetic material—something she's against, mostly for aesthetic reasons—she'd have to cut the fabric entirely with scissors because synthetics don't tear evenly. Also, that material is much harder on the hands than is cotton. Once cut, the long strips are rolled into balls for storage.

Gail prepares the loom for weaving by tying on the warp strings, or "warping the loom." (When the loom is warped, it reminds me of a harp.) The warp strings are the threads which run lengthwise in the rug and are crossed at right angles by the weft, or in Gail's case the strips of rags. For the warp Gail uses a fine cotton twine called "Swedish cotton 12-6"; the numbers refer to 12 bunches of 6 fibers. As she weaves the rug, she joins the

strips together by overlapping the beginning of one strip with the end of the previous one by a few inches. Rugs can be made in any length or width. But because her loom is 4 feet wide, rugs wider than this need to be sewn together in strips.

The patterns and colors the rugs take on reflect Gail's sensitive eye for color. Part of the pleasure in the weaving is deciding on what designs to create. Gail finds inspiration in looking out her studio windows, where she sees continuous changes of colors on Walker's Pond and in the fields behind her house.

In the Winter, Gail often makes braided wool rugs. She can make these in her living room and doesn't need to heat her studio. They are more difficult to make than the rag rugs, since no loom is involved and the weaver must create the tightness in the rug by hand. Usually round or oval, these rugs are made by braiding three strips of wool together and winding the continous braid around and around, lacing the rounds together as one goes. Gail works in her lap, piecing the 2-inch-wide wool strips together and then braiding them. After she prepares a length of braid, she laces it onto the previous round, usu-

ally on a table or on the floor. The wool can be new yardage, or it can be made out of old wool jackets, skirts, trousers, or coats. The colors of these rugs tend to be more muted than the rag rugs, but they are much thicker and warmer.

In addition to making rugs, Gail also spins and knits, which piqued her interest in carding wool. So in 1987, she purchased a huge carding machine, built in 1926, from a mill in Augusta, Maine, with her friend Sarah Christy. The two women set it up in a barn not far from Walker's Pond, where for almost 200 years a water-powered mill had stood. Built in 1768 by Joshua Gray as a grist mill, it was shortly thereafter purchased by John Walker and converted to wool carding. Most of the wool was handspun by Brooksville women and knit into socks and mittens for their families. Local farmers pro-

duced fleece for the mill, which was destroyed by fire in 1962.

Gail and Sarah's carding machine has a series of rollers covered with fine wire teeth, which comb and separate the wool fibers, forming a fine web which can be used for hand spinning, quilt batting, and felting. Gail and Sarah have set up a business called "Walker Pond Carding Mill," for people who want to have their own wool carded.

Our Winter snowstorms can be sudden and fierce (above right): winds howl and the power and phone often go out. In this one, Miso stands guard by the door (above), her Winter fur, full and thick, keeping her warm. Our neighbor Mark came by to have a cup of tea and watch the storm rage, and on his way out, he was nearly blown away (below).

the back door and ski through the woods and fields over the logging roads and hiking trails that crisscross the cape. It was bitter cold at our house, with the wind blowing snow all about, but once in the woods with the trees sheltering us, it was calm and peaceful.

Pausing occasionally to rest and look around us, we could hear the cedar trees creaking and groaning as if to say, "Ah, I didn't think winter was coming in so soon." We could hear the chickadees, but they didn't stay in one place long enough to be spotted. There were lots of rabbit and deer tracks and one set of tracks which were about the size of a small dog's that probably belonged to a coyote. Winter is usually the hardest time of year for these animals, especially when the snowfall is heavy, as it proved to be this year. Just as it is easy for me to follow their tracks, so it is for their predators. We made new tracks since we were the first ones out there, and the going was slow. When we returned home after dark, we sat by the fire and drank hot tea and rum, letting the heat relax us into a dreamy stupor.

While the snow is fresh, before it freezes and thaws, we still have a last chance to harvest our bok choy.

December 10

Coyotes came by the farm yesterday. It was the first time I'd ever seen any in broad daylight, though we'd heard their howling aplenty, mostly at night. They didn't stay around long enough for me to even grab my binoculars. Maybe they were somehow aware that the state of Maine had just this year instituted a bounty law—the "Coyote Award Program." The program offers prizes of $1,500 for the biggest female coyote killed during the year, with $1,000 for the largest male and $1,000 to the one who kills the greatest number of coyotes. Although coyotes do occasionally kill some sheep and may even have killed two of our cats, I still think this animal has become a scapegoat for frustrated hunters; regardless of the bounties, the coyote is here to stay. In fact, studies have shown that where they are intensively hunted and trapped, the size of their litters increases substantially.

Coyotes mate in February and about two months later will whelp in a den. Litters of seven or more pups are not uncommon. The family remains together in the Summer and in the Fall, the young and some of the yearlings find their own territories. Full-grown coyotes appear to be about the size of a small German shepherd, but on average an adult will weigh only 35 pounds. The coyote's ability

During Winter around the farm, the winds can be fierce, making it bitter cold—sometimes down to 20 below zero. But in the woods behind the house, the trees provide a peaceful respite from the wind.

When the air temperature drops to zero and below, sea smoke develops as a result of the great difference between the temperature of the sea water and the air.

to survive is due in part to its ability to exist on a varied diet. Here on the coast of Maine, coyotes devour large quantities of berries in Summer and in Winter become mostly carnivorous, helping to lower the rodent population.

Along with the coyotes, the weather seems to have brought us crows, though we probably notice them more at this time of year. There they were, circling the pond and occasionally lighting in a huge spruce tree near the sauna. They must have been hungry on these cold, gray days when many animals like the skunks, chipmunks, and squirrels have gone into their winter sleep and most of the other birds have flown south. What would they find to eat today in this cold and snow-covered earth? Probably some old bread or rotten apples at the compost pile. Ada Comstock's *Handbook of Nature* paid the crow some compliments. She wrote that the crow is probably the most intelligent of our native birds; it is clever to learn and quick to act. Their resounding cries make me again aware of the silence of this place.

December 13
The cold spell we had for the first two weeks in December set the record for the 110 years that records of the weather have been kept in Maine.. Continued cold

was forecast. This made me especially aware that I had to finish chainsawing up next year's firewood. We keep one year ahead so that the wood can dry out and burn better, with less creosote and danger of chimney fire. We buy the hardwood in 4-foot lengths, cut that into 18-inch lengths, and split it with a maul. Both the stoves in our house are what is referred to as "airtight." They have a baffle inside that does not allow the fire to burn straight up into the stovepipe or chimney. Rather it forces the wood to burn the volatile gases, which burn slower and leave more coals, thereby preserving wood while also burning hotter.

This year we bought seven cords of wood, and it was my job to spend an hour or two a day splitting it. But we've found that two people working together at the woodpile get as much work done as three people alone. One person puts the wood up on the chopping block; the other uses the heavy splitting maul. Consequently, Brett and I trade work on our respective wood piles. Our effort is well worth it. When our stoves are full and next year's woodpile is stacked neatly in the yard, we sleep well.

December 15

Now that recent storms have brought more seaweed into Orr Cove, we plan to collect it as soon as the weather warms up a bit. Since Summer, we've collected eight truckloads and spread it over the gardens as a soil conditioner. This is one of the activities I used to enjoy doing with Scott Nearing, who was always ready to drop what he was doing and go down to the beach, with me driving his truck, to gather up the seaweed. In those days, long fronds of kelp occasionally washed ashore, but mostly we got the knotted wrack or rockweed, with its myriad small air bladders, which grows more abundantly than kelp in our area and is torn loose in the great storms.

In Summer we collect kelp and dry it on the clothesline and pack it away in jars, to be used throughout the year in soups or powdered and sprinkled over rice. Scott was passionate about seaweed and would often proclaim, "Seaweed has all the good things from the land and the sea." And he was right.

Seaweeds are among the most nutritious plants in the world, containing high proportions of proteins, minerals, and vitamins, notably Vitamins A, B1, B12, C, and D. All species of seaweed are rich in minerals and trace elements.

Last Summer's growth on the willow trees adds color to the Winter landscape in front of the house.

Corn bread, made in a cast-iron skillet and sometimes also called spoon bread, is good at any meal.

CORN BREAD

◆

This corn bread has more texture to it because of its whole corn kernels. In a good year, when the coons don't get too much of our corn, Lynn steams the corn and freezes a good amount to use for this recipe through the winter. This dish looks best when presented in a cast-iron skillet, but any ovenproof pan will do. The bread can be spooned out or sliced like a pie. It goes great with maple syrup and a plate of baked beans.

◆

¾ cup yellow corn meal

½ cup rice or white flour

2 teaspoons baking powder

Salt, if desired

1 egg, lightly beaten

2 tablespoons vegetable oil

1 cup milk or soy milk

2 cups frozen corn kernels, thawed

◆

1. Preheat the oven to 350°F. Generously grease a 10-inch cast-iron skillet.

2. In a mixing bowl combine the corn meal, flour, baking powder, and salt to taste. Stir to mix well.

3. In a small bowl, whisk together the egg, oil, and milk.

4. Pour the liquid ingredients into the dry ingredients and stir until just blended; be sure not to overmix. Stir in the corn kernels. Pour the batter into the skillet and bake for 30 to 35 minutes, until the corn bread is browned around the edges and flecked with golden brown on the top. Cut in wedges and serve hot.

Yield: 5 to 6 servings

FLORENE'S BAKED BEANS

◆

Lynn tried many different baked bean recipes, all using salt pork—except Florene's. Hers is our favorite. Florene's Baked Beans are a very hearty treat to fortify the family against those days when it snows and blows. They go well with Dilly Beans and Corn Bread.

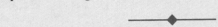

3 cups yellow eye beans or pea beans	¼ cup olive oil
¼ cup molasses	2½ tablespoons dry mustard
¼ cup butter or margarine	1 tablespoon salt

◆

1. Soak the beans overnight in cold water to cover. Or cover the beans with water, bring to a boil and simmer for 2 minutes, then remove them from the heat and let them stand, tightly covered, for 1 hour.

2. Preheat the oven to 250°F. Drain the beans, discarding soaking liquid. In a 3-quart crock or a deep baking dish with a lid, combine the beans with the remaining ingredients. Add enough water to cover the beans by about 1 inch. Cover the dish and bake for 7 to 8 hours, until the beans are tender and have absorbed most of liquid. Stir occasionally, adding more water as needed to keep the beans from getting dry and sticky.

Yield: 6 to 8 servings

Public baked bean suppers held at local churches and grange halls are a Maine tradition beginning in the Fall. A hearty staple of the Winter months, we take them along to potluck dinners.

Gathering seaweed, some of which we eat, some of which we use to fertilize the garden (top), is a year-round occupation, though Winter storms often bring the largest yields. In Summer we hang kelp on the clothes-line to dry before packing it away in air-tight containers to eat throughout the year (above).

Seawater has almost exactly the same proportion of minerals as human blood. One cup of kelp has 2,405mg of calcium—10 times the amount in a glass of milk. It is one of the only foods with iodine. It has 1,670mg of magnesium, or about 300 times the amount in one banana. It also has vast amounts of phosphorus and a 2:1 ratio of potassium to sodium, which is considered very beneficial for human consumption.

December 17

Late yesterday afternoon I went over to Walker's Pond in South Brooksville. Because of the warm Fall, the pond was late to freeze this year, remaining unfrozen at the time of the December 2 snowstorm. Then with the record cold we had for several weeks, it froze fast and as close to perfect as we'll get. It is what's called "black ice."

From some distance, the familiar figure of Larry Packwood advanced toward me. Larry always manages to get out on the good ice a couple of days before me. He can really skate, and after strapping on my skates, I have to work hard to keep up with him. A beautiful scene that must have been, two solitary, tiny figures on that vast pond, gliding under the full yellow moon on black ice as smooth as the smoothest marble. With only the sound of the skate blades on the ice, the hills surrounding the pond outlined against the evening sky, feeling as though we were flying down the wind, gliding over the ice, we experienced a lightness, a feeling of inner peace.

The house was warm when I got back to it. Luckily, there was enough wood in the shed to keep the fires burning, and the root cellar was well enough stocked with bushel baskets of apples, potatoes, turnips, and beets, cabbages and sauerkraut, chutneys and frozen pesto, cider bubbling away in kegs, and bottles of chokecherry and parsnip wine, so that we could get snowed in and never have to go to the store. This is what we work toward the rest of the year.

December 23

Last evening was the darkest of the year, and it was bitter cold—a fitting night to celebrate the Winter solstice with friends: Mark and Mia, Gail, Tom, Emilie, Deirdre, Peter and Jean, Ken and Paula. Though it was only 10 degrees outside, we didn't take long to shed our many layers of winter clothing and settle into the sauna. Ah, the welcome heat. It would take plenty of it to warm our bones, before we climbed down the ladder into the black hole in the pond. Back out of the water in a flash, we felt like children, naked and refreshed. Despite the previous cold spell, only now is Winter officially here.

After the sauna, we celebrated the longest night. We danced around a roaring bonfire, flames arcing high, embers flying thirty feet into the ebony starlit sky, chanting, whooping, to the beat of the huge wooden xylophone. The Amadinda, a figure in a devil's mask, whirled like a dervish amid shouts of "Bring back the sun, bring back the sun." Cups of cider were passed round. Closer to the fire we gathered, until it was down to near ashes, before retreating to the house with good appetite and thirst. The festive kitchen was lit by candles, the two wood stoves fired up against the bitter cold, the table heavily laden with steaming lasagna, crocks of baked beans, cole slaw, various pickles, dilly beans, chutneys, fresh baked breads, fruitcakes, and a macaroon pie.

It was the first day of Hanukkah, the Feast of Lights, and two days before Christmas. We always celebrate both holidays with a large gathering of friends on the 25th. According to Sir James Frazer in *The Golden Bough*:

> In the Julian calender the twenty-fifth of December was reckoned the winter solstice, and it was regarded as the Nativity of the Sun, because the day begins to lengthen and the power of the sun to increase from that turning-point of the year. The ritual of the nativity, as it appears to have been celebrated in Syria and Egypt, was remarkable. The celebrants retired into certain inner shrines, from which at midnight they issued with a loud cry, "The virgin has brought forth! The light is waxing!" The Egyptians even represented the new-born sun by the image of an infant which on his birthday, the winter solstice, they brought forth and exhibited to his worshippers. No doubt the Virgin who thus conceived and bore a son on the 25th of December was the great Oriental goddess whom the Semites called the Heavenly Goddess; in Semitic lands she was a form of Astarte.

From Cape Rosier we can look across Penobscot Bay to the island of Islesboro, and farther to the west, the Camden Hills.

We celebrate the darkest night of the year, the Winter solstice, with a sauna, then dance around a huge bonfire, chanting to the beat of drumming, before escaping into the house for a festive potluck supper.

On the first full day of Winter, the sun rose at 6:56 and set at 3:48, giving us just under nine hours of sunlight. It was still *Sau kalt*, "pig cold" as the Germans say. By then, we had broken all existing records for the coldest December.

Since I had decided to try to plow the snow off the pond, Brett came over in his truck to back me up in case my truck got stuck. Surprisingly, underneath the snow, there was slush; the snow must have insulated the ice almost too well. I wondered if this wasn't madness I was up to. But then I thought, "Well, you only live once." I had the truck on the ice, and I was pushing the snow easily, when suddenly at the far side I felt a thud under me. Heart racing, I threw the truck into reverse. Just by the skin of my teeth, I avoided going into the pond.

I was able to back off onto safe ground, but halfway up the bank of the pond, the truck would go no farther. Brett tried to pull me with his truck, to no avail. We shoveled out under the wheels, the bitter wind reddening our noses, freezing our mittened fingers. Try a "come-along," he advised. Since mine wasn't heavy-duty enough, he went back to his house to get one. Eventually, using his truck as the base from which to pull, I cranked away. But no luck. We gave it one more try with the truck, and finally, straining like a constipated bull, my truck groaned and up she came. I still shudder when I think the truck could have been ten feet under. It was only 10 A.M. and the first day of Winter had begun with a helluva lot more excitement than I had bargained for.

During the long, cold evenings our wood stoves become focal points in the house. We love to roast chestnuts on top of the wood stove in a chestnut pan with special holes in the bottom. After pricking the chestnuts, we let them roast for maybe a half hour until they are soft inside.

December 25

Christmas Day warmed up a bit, but the deep gray sky threatened snow. It was turning dark by 3 P.M. when our guests began arriving. Our friend Gail and her daughters, Emilie and Deirdre, had arrived an hour early to assemble our table's centerpiece—a gingerbread house. Gail and her daughters glued the sides with a sticky caramel made of sugar and water, and they shingled its roof with graham crackers, made doors and shutters of chocolate bars, used red licorice and gumdrops for the fence, and melted lollypops for stained glass windows. Before the house was finally assembled, they placed candles inside and lit them.

When all fourteen guests arrived for our celebration, we trooped out on the icy pond for the annual group photo. Once safely back inside, we assembled in the living room, which glowed in the light from the candlelit tree and from candles set in halved birch logs on the table. Conversation hushed as Tom Hoey's

We enjoy dressing up the house for the holidays. Candles arranged on tables give off a warm glow amid fir boughs and pinecones.

brother Larry presented a Christmas concert of Haydn sonatas and Chopin and Debussy preludes. We sat transfixed, the wood stove crackling away, giving off the smell of balsam fir from the branches we'd set atop it.

Tom loaded the table with bottles of his homemade wines and sparkling cider. He was justifiably proud of his grapewine, since everybody knows you can't get wine grapes to ripen in Maine. Dennis carved the 20-pound turkey, while serving dishes of peas, potatoes, squash, salads, cranberry sauce, and chutneys made their way to the 14-foot table in the living room. We all held hands and observed a minute of silence. Together, we clinked glasses, toasting peace on earth, joy to the world, the cooks, our gathering. The dishes passed, our plates filled, we shared a glorious repast.

After dinner we drank strong coffee. With Emilie at the piano we sang carols, and later Deirdre and Larry offered violin-piano duets. Then Tom read from James Joyce's *Finnegan's Wake*, and Larry capped the evening with another Chopin prelude before everyone departed.

December 26

Today it snowed a couple of inches, enough to make the world look clean and white again, and we went for a cross-country ski around the old logging roads of the cape. Out past Jarvis Green's hunting shacks and through the woods, we went gliding over powdery snow, occasionally following the tracks of the white-tail deer, so easy to distinguish from the others because of the cloven hooves. This has been a hard Winter so far for the deer, for with all the deep, crusty snow they have a hard time getting around. The deer generally bed down in the cedar swamps in the middle of the cape and feed on the buds of deciduous trees and evergreen foliage. Because of this meager diet, combined with the difficulty of movement, they must rely on stored fats to get them through Winter.

Skiing by a clump of low-growing spruce trees, we startled a ruffed grouse (*Bonasa umbellus*, the second part of its Latin name recalling its umbrella-like tail). It returned the favor, flushing and scaring the hell out of me. The ruffed grouse spends most of its time on the ground, and its feet are physically adapted for walking on snow. In Fall, small comblike projections grow on either side of the toes, greatly enlarging the surface area of their feet and supporting them on soft snow. In our area, the bird's Winter diet consists mostly of the buds of poplar and

Michelle Gordon, one of our wreath-makers, gave us a holiday wreath (above) made of bay leaves and rosehips.

We often make fir wreaths with pine cones and holly for family members at this time of year (left).

We decorate every available space at holiday time; here, fir boughs surround old family pictures.

GAIL'S FRUITCAKE

◆

I first tasted Gail Disney's fruitcake about 6 years ago, but somehow never got to baking one myself until this December. It's a great recipe, not nearly as difficult as I'd imagined, and one I plan on making every year from now on. It should be made about a month before Christmas. For hers, Gail buys rolls of marzipan and covers the top of the cake with a thin layer.

◆

2¼ cups all-purpose flour

1 teaspoon ground cinnamon

1 teaspoon ground mixed spice (see Notes)

¼ teaspoon ground nutmeg

1¼ pounds chopped mixed candied fruits (about 3 cups)

12 ounces golden raisins (about 2 cups)

12 ounces currants (about 2 cups)

8 ounces chopped candied citrus peel such as lemon, orange, lime, or a combination (about 1½ cups)

8 ounces pitted and chopped dates (about 1½ cups)

8 ounces chopped dried figs (about 1½ cups)

6 ounces chopped preserved ginger (about 1 cup)

8 ounces coarsely chopped unsalted nuts such as pecans, almonds, or walnuts or a combination (about 2 cups)

8 ounces butter, softened (2 sticks)

1¼ cups packed light-brown sugar

6 eggs

½ cup brandy or rum

½ teaspoon vanilla extract

¼ teaspoon lemon extract

¼ teaspoon almond extract

¼ teaspoon rosewater

12-ounce can crushed pineapple, drained (about 1 cup)

◆

1. Grease 3 loaf pans, line them with waxed paper, and grease the paper. Preheat the oven to 300°F.

2. In a mixing bowl, stir together the flour, cinnamon, mixed spice, and nutmeg. In another very large mixing bowl, toss together the candied fruits, raisins, currants, citrus peel, dates, figs, ginger, and nuts.

3. In the large bowl of an electric mixer, cream the butter with the sugar until light. Beat in the eggs, one at a time, beating well after each addition. With the mixer at low speed, beat in the brandy, vanilla, lemon, and almond extracts and the rosewater alternately with the flour mixture, beating just until well blended. Stir in the pineapple. Pour this batter over the mixed fruits and stir with a large spoon or use your hands to mix the batter thoroughly with the fruits.

4. Divide the batter among the prepared pans, smoothing the tops to level them. Bake them about 2 hours, until a cake tester inserted in the center comes out clean. (If the tops of the fruitcakes begin to brown too much, loosely cover them with aluminum foil for the last 30 minutes of baking.)

5. Cool the cakes in the pans on a rack for 15 minutes, then turn them out of the pans. Carefully peel away the waxed paper and cool the cakes completely. Wrap them in brandy- or rum-soaked cheesecloth, then with aluminum foil. Store at cool temperature in root cellar or in the refrigerator, moistening with more liquor as needed, for about 4 weeks before serving. Serve thinly sliced.

Yield: 3 fruitcakes

Notes: "Mixed spice" is a commercially mixed blend of spices common in England and Ireland. It can be found at some specialty food stores in the United States, but if you can't get it, use equal amounts of ground ginger, cardamom, allspice, and cloves to make the teaspoon required for this recipe.

The fruitcakes can be baked in smaller pans and given as gifts. Each pan should be filled about three-quarters full; baking times will need to be reduced.

When our friends gather for our holiday celebration, we always troop out on the ice for our annual group photo before digging into our Christmas day feast.

Artist and friend Rebeka Raye came over to our house early to make animal dough ornaments for the Christmas tree. After making the dough, she shaped it with her hands and the handle of a spatula, baked it in the oven, and painted it with watercolors and gesso.

beech trees and winterberry leaves. In April, we hear a thumping sound coming from the woods—the mating call of the male grouse, a sound made by drumming wings. We also noticed tiny tracks leading to a rusty, old 55-gallon barrel by the Hunt farm, probably a mouse's house.

January 3

The cold spell snapped on the last day of the year. The temperature rose throughout the morning. By mid-afternoon, it started to rain, the January thaw coming in a day early. Skiing would be out for a while, but we could look forward to good ice for skating. Since the treacherous roads made a group New Year's Eve party impossible, Lynn and I celebrated the year's last night with some broiled salmon steaks and a good bottle of wine. Sipping by the wood stove, we contemplated the end of the decade and anticipated the Winter getaway we make every year: this time to Hawaii.

Living up to our hopes, the ice on Walker's Pond was fine on Sunday, making it possible to spend a couple of hours skating. Near the turn of the century, ice used to be cut from this pond, as it was in many such areas, but the ice they cut here was destined for faraway places. The Maine Lake Ice Company was the largest natural ice plant in the world. Its four giant storage houses could hold 120,000 tons of ice, which would be shipped by huge four- and five-masted schooners to ports in Boston, Baltimore, Washington D.C., the Caribbean, South America, and even India. The schooners, with such names as *Fannie Palmer, Mary F. Barrett,* and the *Gardiner Deering,* were able to dock within a half mile of the plant on Penobscot Bay at the Punch Bowl on Eggemoggin Reach. The 450-pound blocks of ice moved along a conveyor belt to the storage sheds, built of triple construction to provide spaces for air and sawdust insulation between the partitions. But artificial refrigeration brought an end to this important Maine industry, and the ice works closed in 1916.

We kept warm while skating with a thermos of warm buttered rum. A carnival atmosphere prevailed. The ice fishermen were out in force. They had put their tiny warming shacks out on the ice, and groups composed mostly of men drank beer, tended their "pop-ups," and raced around in their three-wheeled ATVs (all-terrain vehicles). They weren't catching much, but that didn't matter. Occasionally, I heard a yelp as someone reeled in a 3-pound bass or a brown

Around the holidays, we decorate our house with all sorts of treasures. The tree is lit with candles (left) and trimmed with handmade dough ornaments, tin ornaments from Mexico, and old glass balls we've collected through the years. Around the doorways (above), we hang garlands of ribbons, fir branches, gingerbread men, and airplanes—reminders of Lynn's hobby.

CARVING DECOYS

I've always admired wood carving, so I was delighted to meet George Hardy, a lifetime local resident and a still husky and vigorous 73, who has begun making a name for himself as a wood carver. His reputation has grown, along with his menagerie, since he retired five years ago from building chimneys and foundations. Now he carves and sells colorful wooden creatures full-time. His shop is full of yellow cats with bright red tongues, aquamarine alligators with huge teeth, 5-foot-long black snakes with yellow stripes, fish hawks or osprey, puffins, lots of seagulls mounted on driftwood, loons, cormorants—or, as George calls them, shag—woodpeckers, deer, a black and white cow with four pink teats and deer antlers, a family of zebras, and a beady-eyed porcupine.

When I come into his shop for a visit, he tells me, "Can't sell a duck anymore. Now they want rabbits and dogs." Pointing to the 4-foot-long version of Noah's ark he's working on, he adds, "This'll go for $600. Man from New York ordered it." With the large boat comes an array of animals—skunks, zebras, sheep, giraffes, bears, a goldfinch, two yellow ducks down in the hold—and, of course, Noah.

Standing near the ark is a 3-foot-tall Indian with a rifle, still in need of a coat of paint. George says a man came in the other day and wanted him to do an Indian woman, which he said would be no problem. "Half the time they want what I ain't got," he remarks. He points at a howling coyote painted blue and says, "Lady from New Jersey wanted that and I shouda got a deposit. Don't know if she'll be back."

George started out carving duck decoys, which hunters would buy to attract ducks in the Fall. One day, a Summer resident stopped in and asked if he could make her a sea gull. George didn't see why not. Well, one sea gull led to another, and pretty soon more folks were stopping by asking for cats, snakes, pigs, roosters —even deer.

George has come a long way from the decoys to his present-day piebald collection.

His workshop is full of chunks of wood in varying sizes, which he says need to dry out before he works with them. It will take anywhere from three to five years for them to be dry enough so that they won't check, or crack, after being carved.

Pine, which is George's favorite because it's easy to carve, is getting scarce and expensive. "But I've got a good supply of it," he reports. "Just the other day I went up to Banga and bought me a truckload of scrap pine from a log cabin company. It's green wood though, and it'll take years to dry before I can use it."

All the animals are made from patterns, which hang from the low ceiling in his workshop. There are boxes and boxes of sandpaper and a large bandsaw. George traces the outline of the pattern onto a piece of dried pine and then cuts it out on the bandsaw. I ask George where he gets the ideas for his animals since they are more colorful and fanciful than one would encounter in the wild. "Why, from my head, where else," he retorts.

Once roughed out, he works the refinements in with a jackknife, adding eyes, which he buys from a company in Texas. After sanding, the piece is given a coat of white oil-based primer and then painted with oil-based paint. George appears to be among friends when he's with his animals and birds, but it's getting late in the afternoon and Mr. Hardy is ready to close up shop. He tells me with a glint in his eye, "The wife's got the beans on."

Before I depart, I notice a sign over one of the birds: "All fishermen are damn liars except you and me, and sometimes I'm not so sure about you."

When the ice on Walker's Pond is in good condition, a carnival atmosphere prevails. Here, Emilie laces up her skates; the kids enjoy an old-fashioned sled; and the ice boats are a new fascination for us. Brian is getting a running start for his two-man Hudson River–type ice boat.

Even after snowstorms in December, there are still some healthy kale leaves to harvest from the Winter garden.

trout. Elmer Lymnbyrner, one of the fishermen, said he was using "shiners" (a type of minnow) for bait and that it could be fairly costly to set up to go ice fishing. "See that auga over theya?" he asked. "That was $250, and my cousin Sunny bought an ice tent for $120. And these pop-ups ain't cheap. Some of them cost as much as sixteen bucks each at the stoa, and Basil bought a portable fishin' shelter for a hundred bucks. I made my own shack outa scrap I got from the dump. Ayah," he concluded as I nodded and skated off.

A couple of trucks drove out on the ice and roared up and down the nearly two-mile-long pond. But most exciting to me were the iceboats, two small single ones and a large two-person "Hudson River" type. In the two-person boat, which has a mainsail and a small jib sail and iron blades, the passenger lies on his or her stomach facing the front, holding onto the mainsail sheet, while the driver has his head to the stern and controls the tiller. The boat can easily go 50 miles per hour. I had a thrilling ride on one, with my face only a foot and a half from the ice as we "tore ass," as they say around here. My adrenalin must have been pumping furiously away; it was frightening and exhilarating at the same time. Next November I hope to build one of the smaller boats.

Throughout Fall and Winter, I make sourdough rye bread (above and opposite). The kitchen cabinets behind me (top) are handpainted with scenes of peasant life by Mary Stackhouse, who owned our farm before Scott and Helen Nearing.

SOURDOUGH RYE BREAD

Friends used to call my very dense sour rye bread "chain saw bread" because after it sat a few days you'd practically need a chain saw to cut it. But I've changed the recipe a little and now "steam" the bread while it's baking, so it's not so hard to cut. Through the years I've tried adding fruit and nuts to my recipe and now have a good variation. When friends stop by we take out the bread and hard cider, and maybe some sharp New England cheddar.

Follow these proportions only if you can get flour made from rye berries ground on a hand-operated grain mill. Commercial rye flour—or even flour from berries freshly ground in an electric mill—is much finer than the hand-ground flour I use. Hand-milled flour is very coarse and flavorful. Rye berries are available at health food stores and in shops that offer organic ingredients. Commercial rye flour absorbs much larger amounts of liquid; if you are working with it, plan to use a lot more water.

Sourdough starter:

> *1 tablespoon dry yeast*
>
> *2½ cups warm water*
>
> *2 teaspoons sugar or honey*
>
> *2½ cups coarse rye flour*

Bread:

> *1 cup sourdough starter*
>
> *6½ cups coarse rye flour (ground from about 2 pounds rye berries in a hand-operated grain mill)*
>
> *3½ cups warm water*
>
> *2 to 3 cups unbleached white flour*
>
> *1 tablespoon salt*
>
> *3 to 4 tablespoons caraway seeds, or to taste*

To make the starter, in a ceramic bowl, mix all the ingredients together with a wooden spoon until smooth and blended. Cover with a damp cloth and set aside in a warm, draught-free spot for 3 or 4 days, when the mixture will be bubbly and slightly sour. To store the starter, cover tightly and refrigerate.

1. In a large ceramic bowl, combine the sourdough starter, rye flour, and water. With a wooden spoon, stir until smooth. This is the "sponge," which should be a loose batter. Cover the bowl well with plastic wrap, making sure a tight seal is formed. Set it aside in a warm place—preferably 75° to 80°F —for 4 days, or until the sponge is bubbly and has acquired a pleasant sour smell. Remove and reserve 1 cup of the sponge, tightly covered, to use as the starter for the next batch of bread and store in glass or ceramic container in refrigerator.

2. Stir in about 2 cups of the white flour, along with the salt and caraway seeds. Turn the dough out onto a floured board and knead it with floured hands for about 10 minutes, adding additional flour so dough is soft but workable.

3. Preheat the oven to 300°F. Bring about a quart of water to a boil and allow to simmer. Lightly grease 2 baking sheets or 3 loaf pans and dust them with cornmeal. Divide the dough into 2 or 3 pieces and shape them into oval or round loaves or loaves for the bread pans. Transfer the loaves to the prepared sheets or pans and diagonally slash the tops with a sharp knife in 3 places.

4. Place the bread on the upper oven rack. On the lower rack, place a bread pan and fill it with boiling water to create steam, which helps to produce a good crust and moist bread. Bake the bread for 60 to 80 minutes, or until it is nicely browned and has a hollow sound when tapped on the bottom.

5. Cool the bread on racks. Cut into thin slices for serving.

FRUITED RYE BREAD

◆

1 recipe Sourdough Rye Bread
*   dough, omitting the caraway*
*   seeds*

½ cup molasses

About ½ teaspoon nutmeg

2½ to 3 pounds chopped dried
*   fruit and unsalted nuts*
*   any combination of figs,*
*   golden raisins, currants,*
*   dates, hazelnuts, pecans, and*
*   sunflower seeds (6 to 7 cups)*

━━━━━━━━━◆━━━━━━━━━

Follow the instructions above, stirring in the molasses, nutmeg, fruits, and nuts along with the white flour and salt in step 2. Because of the molasses, you will probably need the larger amount of flour.

Yield: 4 or 5 loaves for each recipe

On our way south, we visit Brian and Louise. Here, they look on in wonder as their goose Toulouse flies off their porch.

January 20

Toward the end of the year and into the new one, the seed catalogs come pouring in. Besides the tomatoes and beans, lettuce and peppers which have done well for us in the past, we always try some new ones to add to the excitement of the coming seasons. Johnny's Selected Seeds, located here in Maine, has an informative catalog and often interesting new varieties of vegetables. We order our onion sets, French filet beans, Chinese greens, and clover cover crops from them. But Stokes, located in Buffalo, New York, with their long experience and good prices, gets most of our vegetable seed business. Stokes sells thirty varieties of cucumbers, and four pages of their catalog are devoted to different kinds of corn.

Thompson and Morgan, with their color photos, lure me in. They seem to have both the most extensive and the most expensive offering of flowers. In addition to the usual asters, dahlias, and cosmos, we ordered a new variety of delphinium, "Pink Dream," which comes thirty seeds for $4.40, and a variety of columbine, "Flabellata," nodding lilac-blue and cream flowers from Japan. Sixteen of these valuable seeds sell for $3.30. We also ordered another columbine, "Caerulea," which has deep blue flowers and is the state flower of Colorado; a variety of *Polemonium* or Jacob's ladder called "Blue Pearl," which blooms in early summer; and another early-bloomer, *Linum* or flax.

More catalogs pour in from Burpee, Gurney's, Park, Shepherds. The Cook's Garden in Londonderry, Vermont, always seems to excite us with their unusual seeds from Europe and Japan. So we'll try some mizuna, a Japanese mustard, which has the feathery look of peacock kale, and a type of escarole, "Cornet d'Anjou," named for its horn shape and its home in Anjou, France. Cook's Garden lists nine varieties of basil, and in addition to "Piccolo Verde Fino," we decide to try "Purple Ruffles," with its deeply cut foliage and an intense purple color. We also ordered "Fin de Bagnols," a gourmet green bean.

The color photography in the White Flower Farm catalog is so enticing that I begin making lists of plants I would like to have for the coming year: begonias, lilies—maybe one called "Alpenglow" which they describe as having 7-inch blooms in a shade of rose-pink with magenta spots—astilbe, Japanese iris, hostas, *Perovskia* or Russian sage, and much more. St. Lawrence Nurseries, specializing in organically grown fruit and nut trees, guaranteed to be hardy for our severe northern winters, offers at least a hundred varieties of apple trees and many pear, plum, butternut, chestnut, and black walnut trees. Each year, we make sure to plant several fruit trees.

February 3

Our seeds are ordered. The wood for next year is cut and split. The tools have been oiled and sharpened, and Dottie Gray's daughter Sammy will be staying here to keep the fires going and give the cats some needed company. They will miss us. Amazingly, they always know when we are going away.

Migrating south only for two months, we'll be back in time to give our seedlings the jump start they need in this climate. Our return is timed before the Canada geese fly northward in late March, reminding us of the renewing cycle of planting, growing, and harvesting that has become the focus of our lives.

AFTERWORD

Scott Nearing died in 1983 at the age of one hundred. Now in her eighty-sixth year, Helen still lives in excellent health in a stone house next to ours and is considering spending her last years in Holland. She is working on her auto-biography and would prefer not to sell her home, to keep it from becoming a "Summer place." She is hoping to find the right couple to hand it over to.

Her stone house is solid and austere. It feels something like a monastery, a place of meditation and serious work. She is still very active and enjoys telling visitors that she was in her seventies and Scott was in his nineties when they began to build their house in 1973. I asked Helen what she would do differently if she could do it over again. "Not a darn thing," she says.

Now our small peninsula is in transition. Developers have subdivided the four hundred acres bordering our land into forty lots, and million-dollar houses are going up. Roads have been cut all over the land the Penobscot Indians once roamed and hunted, and the sound of chainsaws often destroys our silence. But we still have the community which has surrounded the farm since the Nearings started selling nearby land to young homesteaders in 1968. Fourteen people in eight houses now live here—carpenters, cabinetmakers, gardeners, a dancer and her husband, a blacksmith. The cape is covered with old logging roads, and there is a hiking trail which connects all of us who live on the Nearing's old land.

We have our communal saunas and, with them, try to retain a sense of group sharing. We have heated debates about what we should do with the skunk caught in a Hav-a-Heart trap and whether the porcupine has the right to chew down the two-year-old apple tree or the lush raspberry bushes. We observe the ancient celebrations of the solstices with communal bonfires, dancing to the beat of the Amadinda.

Life on the Maine coast is hard, but it is a good life, a quality life, a way of living simply in troubled times. When Scott was ninety-five, I heard him give a lecture at the Common Ground Fair in Litchfield, Maine. He talked about gardening and homesteading, and concluded by telling the audience, "If you want to have a garden, just go out and do it. Just go out and do it." I've often heard those words as I think about taking on a new project or expanding the gardens. Despite any divergence from Scott's philosophy and practice Lynn and I have taken as we made the Maine farm ours, that too would be my best advice to anyone thinking about creating a new kind of life for themselves: "Just go out and do it!"

ACKNOWLEDGMENTS

We are greatly indebted to our family, friends, and neighbors for helping us along the path to this book. We had love and support from my mother, my brother Jay and his wife Susan, Lynn's parents, Florence and Sy Karlin, and her sister Gail Marks.

Over many years Helen and Scott Nearing inspired people like ourselves to live in the country.

It was our editor, John Smallwood, who encouraged us to do this book, and through his guidance and cheerful, positive approach the book took shape.

We want to acknowledge those who are special in our lives:

Brett Brubaker, friend, neighbor, "house doctor," and horseshoe buddy for always being there to help us out through the years.

Our friends: Gail Disney and Tom Hoey, Sherry Streeter and Jon Wilson, Jean Gaudette and Peter Diemond, Mia Kanazawa and Mark Kindschi, Deb Marshall and Kim Petty, Ken Woisard, Rufus Hellendale, Kathie and Jack Burnett, Jean and Dud Hendrick and their staff at the Pilgrim's Inn.

Our Summer friends who have been so encouraging through the years: Paul and Jean Lewis, Dan and Liz Hoffman, and the Razi and Krody families. And friends farther away: Meindert Brouwer, Steve Hanson, Steve Cote and Julie Stiler, Brian Winn and Louise Jaubert, Marcel Meijer and Diane Torr, Lori Hanson and Mike Smith, and Mike Faye and Susan Duncan.

The children who bring such energy and joy when they come to visit: Emilie and Deirdre, Plumi and Gigi, Martina, Ollie, Faye, and Ella, Gregory and Virginia, and all the others.

Our helpers who have made beautiful wreaths over the years: Joanna Donaldson, Rebecca Elder, Mia Kanazawa, Michelle Gordon, Doris Groves, Meredith and Andrea DeFrancesco, and all the rest.

Lynn wishes to acknowledge her pilot friends: Dud Hendrick, Charlie Smith, Debbie Larrabee, Paul Brayton, and Bob Hitchcock for taking over the controls when she did the aerial photographs.

I am grateful to Paul Lewis for his good work editing the early manuscript, to Katherine Razi for her spirited and animated help, and to Wendy Batteau, who asked a thousand questions in a fine job of editing.

And finally the Holy Mackerels, Akiwabas, our cat family—Miso, Gesso, Picasso, Pistachio, Willow, Gusto, Wheezo, and Gaspacho—and all the other friends and neighbors who have been part of our lives on Cape Rosier, we are most grateful.

Smallwood and Stewart would like to add their thanks to Cathie Revland for her creative assistance with the manuscript, Susan E. Davis for shepherding this book through its final stages, and Dianna Russo and Suzanne Lincoln for their work on the layouts.

resources

Baldwin Kayaks
Earl Baldwin
R.F.D. #2, Box 268
Orrington, ME 04474
Handmade fiberglass
and Kevlar kayaks

Cape Rosier Wreaths
R.R. Box 12
Harborside, ME 04642
Dried-flower wreaths

Clarkpoint Croquet Co.
P.O. Box 457
Southwest Harbor, ME 04679
Handcrafted croquet sets

The Cook's Garden
P.O. Box 65
Londonderry, VT 05148
Vegetable seeds

Gail Disney
Box 24
South Brooksville, ME 04617
Handwoven rag rugs

George Hardy
Box 129
Deer Isle, ME 04627
Hand-carved decoys

Johnny's Selected Seeds
Albion, ME 04910
Flower and vegetable seeds

Kelco Industries
Milbridge, ME 04658
Source of our wreath rings
and wire

The Necessary Catalog
P.O. Box 305
New Castle, VA 24127
Wide selection of organic fertilizers,
cover crops, pest controls

St. Lawrence Nurseries
R.D. 2
Potsdam, NY 13676
Specializes in growing cold-hardy
fruit and nut trees

Shepherds Garden Seeds
30 Irene St.
Torrington, CT 06790
Vegetable seeds, especially
salad vegetables

Smith and Hawkin
25 Corte Madera
Mill Valley, CA 94941
Garden tools, clothing, and bulbs

Sow's Ear Cider
Box 24
South Brooksville, ME 04617'
Organic cider made in English
style from unsprayed wild apples;
available locally

Stokes Seeds Inc.
Box 548
Buffalo, NY 14240
Flower and vegetable seeds

Thompson & Morgan
P.O. Box 1308
Jackson, NJ 08527
Flower and vegetable seeds

White Flower Farm
Litchfield, CT 06759-0050
Wide range of hardy perennials,
shrubs, Spring flowering bulbs

bibliography

Beston, Henry. *Northern Farm: A Chronicle of Maine*. Camden, Me.: Down East Books, 1948.

Britton, Nathanial Lord, and Hon, Addison. *An Illustrated Flora of the Northern United States and Canada*. New York: Dover Publications, Inc., 1970.

Complete Field Guide to North American Wildlife. Eastern Edition. New York: Harper & Row, 1981.

Field Guide to the Birds of North America. Washington, D.C.: National Geographic Society, 1987.

Frazer, Sir James George. *The Golden Bough*. New York: Collier Books, Macmillan Publishing Company, 1963.

Gibbons, Euell. *Stalking the Wild Asparagus*. Putney, Vt.: Alan C. Hood, 1962.

Grieve, Maude. *A Modern Herbal*. New York: Dover Publications, Inc., 1971.

Nearing, Helen and Scott. *Living the Good Life*. New York: Schocken Books, 1972.

————. *Continuing the Good Life: Half a Century of Homesteading*. New York: Shocken Books, 1979.

Peterson, Roger Tory. *A Field Guide to the Birds*. Boston: Houghton Mifflin Company, 1947.

Proulx, Annie, and Nichols, Lew. *Sweet and Hard Cider*. Charlotte, Vt.: Garden Way Publishing, 1980.

Rich, Louise Dickinson. *The Coast of Maine*. New York: Thomas Y. Crowell Company, 1962.

Rodale, J. I. *How to Grow Vegetables and Fruits by the Organic Method*. Emmaus, Pa.: Rodale Books, Inc., 1961.

Smith, Alexander H. *The Mushroom Hunter's Field Guide*. Ann Arbor: The University of Michigan Press, 1977.

Stokes, Donald W. *A Guide to Nature in Winter. Northeast and North Central America*. Boston: Little, Brown and Company, 1976.

White, E. B. *Essays of E. B. White*. New York: Harper & Row, 1979.

Wyman, Donald. *Wyman's Gardening Encyclopedia*. New York: Macmillan Publishing Company, 1977.